D1572418

Following The Drum

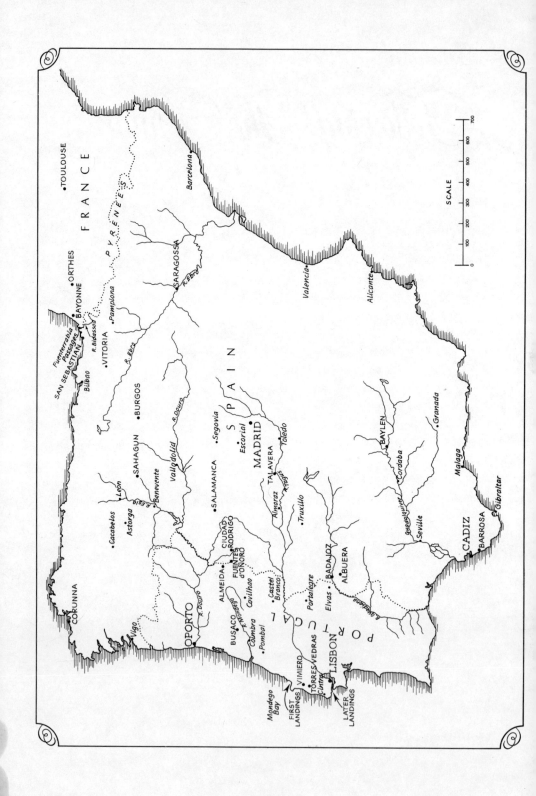

Following The Drum

WOMEN IN WELLINGTON'S WARS

BRIGADIER F.C.G. PAGE

ANDRE DEUTSCH

First published 1986 by
André Deutsch Limited
106 Great Russell Street London WC1

Page, F.C.G.
Following the drum : women in Wellington's
wars
1. Great Britain. *Army* —— History
2. Napoleonic Wars, 1800-1814 —— Campaigns
3. Camp followers —— History —— 19th
century 4. War —— Women's work ——
History —— 19th century
I. Title
940.2'7   DC202

ISBN 0 233 97960 3

Phototypeset by Falcon Graphic Art Ltd
Wallington, Surrey
Printed in Great Britain by
Ebenezer Baylis & Son Ltd
Worcester

CONTENTS

ACKNOWLEDGEMENTS

I would like to thank the Mansell Collection for permission to reproduce illustrations 1, 2, 3, 4, 5, 6, 7, 8, 11, 12 and 13, and the National Army Museum, London, for permission to reproduce illustrations 9, 10, 14, 15, 16, 20 and 21. Illustrations 17 and 18 are taken from *A Week at Waterloo* by Lady de Lancey. I am particularly grateful to the trustees of the Goodwood Estate for very kindly providing the print of the Waterloo Ball painting by R. D. Willingford, and for generously allowing me to reproduce it.

I also wish to thank the following publishers for their kind permission to quote from copyright works: Michael Joseph for *The Letters of Private Wheeler*; Hodder and Stoughton for *The Gasgoyne Heiress*; Hutchinson and Company for *Sir John Moore's System of Training*; Weidenfeld and Nicholson for *Wellington, The Years of the Sword*; and the Longman Group for *The Wheatley Diary*.

I am more than grateful to Lady Longford, the distinguished historian, for providing such a delightful foreword.

I would also like to thank my publishers for the invaluable help they have given me in the production of the book.

Finally, I would like to express my gratitude to Miss Jennifer Brain, who selected the illustrations and without whose help, advice and encouragement the book would never have been submitted for publication.

FOREWORD

If ever there were a fitting tribute to women's courage in adventure and adversity, this book is it. Women who actually *fought* in wars have been worthily dealt with elsewhere. But what of those many thousands who simply accompanied their husbands to the front? Brigadier Page's short but wonderfully comprehensive book fills a real gap. Few stories of devotion, suffering and romance can rival the ones so movingly yet factually told here.

In her much acclaimed study, *Monuments and Maidens*, Marina Warner points out that sculpted virtues like Justice and Liberty are always represented as women, even the ones that might claim to be essentially male. Courage, on the Victoria Memorial at one end of the Mall, is a woman with wings. At the other end of the Mall, on Admiralty Arch, a monument to Gunnery shows one woman with a sextant in her lap, another woman nursing a miniature cannon as if it were a baby. In this book we shall find actual not allegorical mothers nursing their infants almost in the cannon's mouth.

The chapters are structured with military precision. Beginning with guidelines to Wellington's Peninsular War and its delayed climax at Waterloo, we move on to the general conditions in which soldiers' wives existed when campaigning. And very shocking most of them were; though the wives' heroic determination not to be left behind means that the tale is seldom one of unrelieved gloom. Particularly interesting is the account of how lots were drawn for the 'lucky' wives – and children – permitted to board the British transports for Spain and Portugal. Only six – later only four – applicants were allowed to every hundred soldiers in a regiment. One can imagine the screams of anguish at the docks of those wives who had drawn a 'Not-to-go' ticket, and the ecstasy, often misplaced, of those with a ticket marked 'To-go'. Imagination is aided by a print of a 'Not-to-go' wife and her children saying farewell to their man, one of the many lively contemporary prints that illustrate the text.

Once in Spain and Portugal, a kaleidoscope of deftly sketched vignettes illumines the various opportunities and perils which awaited the successful wives. Their main occupation, apart from donkey-riding or sheer trudging across Spain, was cooking, and mending and laundering their husbands' clothes, perhaps earning extra pennies by washing for batchelor soldiers also. Most wives were content to *follow* the drum. But a few tough wives, or girl-friends picked up en route, would beat the drum to it. Wellington had to issue an order preventing women from getting ahead and buying up the available bread in a village before the commissaries could reach it.

The Brigadier is too much of a gentleman to mention more than once the wives who disgraced themselves, along with their husbands, by drinking themselves to death, or into stupor or captivity. Rightly he emphasises their almost incredible hardships: lost children, babies born by the wayside on the line of march, foreign lovers sold and re-sold, wives widowed and widowed again, near starvation in frozen or scorched-earth country. Brigadier Page aptly compares the retreat to Corunna to a mini-retreat from Moscow.

As the book progresses the human dramas become fuller, more detailed, more compelling, until we wind up with the well-documented romances of Harry and Juana Smith and Magdalene and William de Lancey. I can add one happy ending to the many tales of love and sacrifice, elopement and betrayal. Among the British Peninsular forces were Protestant men who fell in love with Catholic Spanish or Portuguese girls; their families understandably objected. Wellington saved one such girl from a convent-prison. A few years ago I received a letter from the girl's great-great-great-great-granddaughter saying that the couple had married and their family had lived happily in Portugal ever after.

This poignant series of short stories and sketches is not exactly an addition to feminist literature. Nevertheless it achieves with truthfulness and persuasive charm what others have sometimes failed to do by force and fury: put thousands of hitherto unknown, humble women on to the map of humanity.

Elizabeth Longford

INTRODUCTION

Too often the history of war is condensed into a list of battles and dates. Mention is made of the senior commanders but little, if anything, is said of the junior officers and the men who did the fighting. Still less is known of the role of women in war. Indeed, the vast majority of general readers are unaware that in the Duke of Wellington's time it was the custom for each regiment to be accompanied by a number of wives when it left England to go to war.

In September 1799 a British expedition was despatched under the Duke of York to fight the French in Holland. Lady Bessborough, who was then staying in Margate, made a number of visits to the pier to watch the embarkation. The bustle and excitement appealed to her sense of adventure and she wrote to her friend, Lord Leveson Gower, 'The cheer given by the soldiers and answered by the mob at the moment they sail is the most affecting thing possible, when one considers how often it must be a farewell for ever.'[1] At the same time she was sad to see the young men sailing away to face danger abroad and she was particularly affected by 'the numbers of young women crying and taking leave of them'.

One day she noticed a young mother weeping bitterly. The unhappy girl had an infant in her arms and a small child, about a year old, stood beside her. It was easy to see that her husband was among those going to the war and that she was to be left behind. When the men were all aboard and the anchor had been raised, the ship started to edge slowly forwards. As it neared the pierhead the young woman pushed her way to the front of the crowd of friends and relations who were waving their last farewells. Then, seeing her husband looking towards her, she made a last desperate effort

I

to accompany him to the war. She first threw the elder child into his arms, then, still clutching her baby tightly, she herself jumped on to the moving ship. This courageous act was received with great enthusiasm by the crowd on shore who cheered loudly and shouted their approval. The soldiers on board, kind as British soldiers always are to those in distress, quickly made a space for the girl and laid her down on the deck so that she might recover her composure. Fortunately, the officer in charge was so impressed by her courage and determination that, despite the strict rules limiting the number of women who could accompany the men, she was allowed to remain on board with her husband.[2]

On another occasion, Lady Bessborough singled out two very pretty young women who were bidding farewell to a junior officer. When he went on board and turned to kiss his hand to them, one hid her head in the bosom of the other and burst into uncontrollable sobs. Lady Bessborough was so overcome that she had difficulty in restraining her own tears. She could not understand how the wives and sweethearts could bear to stay behind. She decided that had it been she, somehow she would have contrived to sail with the army. Another young wife who was embarking with the troops that day felt the same. When asked how she could face such a prospect she quickly replied, 'I could not think of staying; I have been moving Heaven and earth ever since I heard of it and if I had not succeeded in getting leave to go with him, I would have followed in the first fishing boat that would take me.'[3]

Following the Drum tells the stories of courageous women such as these, who accompanied Wellington's armies as they fought their way across the Spanish Peninsula and into France in 1808 to 1815, pushing back the occupying French troops. They chose to subject themselves, and often their children, to the rigours and horrors of war in order that they might not be separated from their loved ones. None of these women actually served in Wellington's armies. The women's services had not been conceived of at that time. Indeed, in those days the very idea was inconceivable. On the other hand, it was permitted that the troops be accompanied by a large entourage of wives, who were joined, as the campaign wore on, by numerous Spanish and Portuguese girls, some of whom married British soldiers and some of whom followed the army without benefit of clergy. Those men who were single or had not been able

2

to bring their wives along, did not take long to discover the charms of the local ladies. Their first contact with the Spanish Peninsula was in Portugal, where they found that 'the middle-sized, plump form, black, bright and expressive eyes, and regular teeth of a dazzling brightness, are the peculiar characteristics of the beauty of a Portuguese female, and constitute here as they would anywhere else, a very pretty woman.'[4] Moving into Spain, 'the large black eye, the dark, expressive glance, the soft, blood-tinged olive of the glowing complexion, make the unwilling Englishman confess the majesty of Spanish beauty, and he feels that though the soft blue eye, the delicate loveliness of his own countrywomen awaken more sensitive feelings of interest, he would deny, or dispute, in vain the commanding superiority of these dark-eyed and fine-formed damsels.'[5] Finally, in France, the victorious army had the fun 'of making love to the pretty little girls with which the place abounded'.[6]

But there was more than one view as to whether women should have been there at all. Although James Anton, Quartermaster of the 42nd Foot, was happily married and took his wife to the war, he was, nevertheless, of the opinion that it would have been better if the authorities had arranged for the proper accommodation in England for the families of soldiers on active service, so that their children would grow up with roots in their own towns and villages.[7] However, most of the men thought otherwise. The general view was that the women were a great asset, not only as cooks, laundrywomen and seamstresses, but as companions who humanized the hard life of the camps. J. Kincaid, an officer in the 95th Rifles, complained that when there were no women with the regiment, 'the ceremony of washing a shirt amounted to a servant's taking it by the collar and giving it a couple of shakes in the water, and then hanging it up to dry.'[8] The less practical Major Sherer, who went to the Peninsula in the 48th Foot and was taken prisoner in 1813, valued the ladies more for their society than their domestic skills. For him a plentiful supply of tea, sugar, brandy and 'segars' was no substitute for the lack of books and the company of women.

There can be no doubt that the women did create a number of administrative and disciplinary problems for the staff. Nevertheless, it is safe to say that despite these difficulties their presence was

a potent factor in the maintenance of morale and made a contribution to victory that has not always been recognized.

The chapters which follow will attempt to set the record straight.
They will tell how these women found their way to the war, of their
life at sea on the troopships and how they fared on the march, in
camp and in battle. The book consists in the main of a number of
short stories culled from the diaries and memoirs of men who
fought in Wellington's campaigns. They form a patchwork which,
when pieced together, may give the reader some idea of the life of
the ladies who followed the drum. For those who are unfamiliar
with the history of the period, the first chapter provides a brief
chronological account of Wellington's campaigns as a background
to the events described in the body of the book.

Chapter

ONE

WELLINGTON'S CAMPAIGNS

IN 1807 Britain and France had been at war for fourteen years. During this period the French had successively defeated all the continental armies of Europe, but the British had remained supreme at sea. In spite of their successes the French had never been able to negotiate a prolonged peace as fresh coalitions continued to be formed against them. This was largely because of the financial subsidies and encouragement given by the British government. The British were able to provide substantial sums to their allies from the profits they made from their foreign trade. Napoleon realized that to preserve his control of the continent he would have to stop these payments and to do this it would be necessary to destroy the British seaborne carrying trade. As he could not prevent the movement of merchant ships on the high seas, he issued the Berlin Decrees forbidding the landing of British merchandise in any continental port. In spite of this, British goods continued to arrive and to receive a wide distribution in European countries. Much was brought in by smugglers, but in Portugal the flouting of Napoleon's orders was more flagrant. The Portuguese Prince Regent refused to submit to the Decrees and Portuguese trade with the British continued to be carried on openly. In an angry reaction Napoleon sent an army under General Junot to occupy Lisbon, where it arrived in December 1807. In spite of this threat the Prince Regent refused to declare war on England and escaped to Brazil with his family, escorted by a squadron of the British navy.

During the invasion of Portugal, at which the Spanish government had connived, nearly 100,000 French troops had flooded into Spain. Using these as a demonstration of his power, Napoleon was able to compel the Spanish royal family to surrender the throne in the Treaty of Bayonne, in favour of his elder brother, Joseph. Such treachery was more than Spanish pride could bear. In a wave of patriotic fervour men flocked to join both the regular army, which was far from efficient, and, more significantly, to form themselves into highly effective guerrilla bands that were to render invaluable service in the ensuing war. Though the central government had ceased to function, the provincial *juntas* sent emissaries to England asking for assistance. They were promised money, arms and the support of a British expeditionary force. This force sailed for Corunna on 12 July 1808. Sir Arthur Wellesley, who was in command, went ahead of his convoy in a fast frigate. On arrival in the north of Spain he found the Spaniards in an excited mood. General Castanos had defeated a French force at Baylen and captured 18,000 prisoners, while General Palafox was conducting a successful defence of Saragossa with a largely civilian garrison. Under these circumstances they were delighted to receive British cash and arms, but in a mood of misplaced confidence were less keen on accepting British troops. Wellesley was advised to land in Portugal. After further consultations it was decided to disembark on open beaches near the mouth of the Mondego river. This operation, which commenced on 1 August, was carried out in a heavy swell, causing several boats to be swamped and some men to be drowned.

After a rapid advance in the direction of Lisbon, Wellesley defeated the French at Vimiero, and General Junot agreed by the terms of the Convention of Cintra, on 31 August, to evacuate Portugal without further resistance. The terms of the Convention, which were considered to be too lenient, were severely criticized in England. Wellesley returned home to defend his actions at a Court of Enquiry, and the command of the army passed to Sir John Moore. Sir John was a popular general and a favourite of HRH the Duke of York, then commander-in-chief of the British army. He was renowned for his courage and had made a great reputation both as a subordinate general in action and for original thought when in charge of the training camp at Shorncliffe. He had, however, no experience of being in supreme command in the field, was pessimistic by nature and tended to be indecisive. He made a quick advance into Spain, but then delayed for a valuable month at Salamanca. By this time the Spanish armies, lacking any central control, had been defeated and dispersed. Moore, feeling that he was in honour bound to take some action against the French, attempted a thrust against their lines of communication. On discovering that his army was hopelessly outnumbered by a much stronger force than his own under the command of Napoleon in person, he decided to withdraw through the Galician mountains to Corunna. In an ill-conducted retreat the morale of his army broke down to such an extent that one of his generals wrote, 'We resembled more a crowd of insubordinate rebels in full flight than a corps of British troops in the presence of an enemy.' The suffering of the women and children was appalling. On the heights above Corunna the army rallied and occupied a position to cover the embarkation. When the pursuing French attacked, Sir John Moore was killed, but Sir John Hope, who took over command, successfully withdrew the army to the ships. After a stormy passage the men arrived in England, dirty, ragged and dis-organized.

This reverse was a great blow to British morale at home, particularly as Moore had declared that far from being able to retain possession of Portugal the British army would not be able to hold Lisbon against the French. However, the government, in the face of much opposition, showed great courage in continuing to support the Spanish by sending more supplies of money and arms and by the despatch of a second expeditionary force to Portugal under the command of Sir Arthur Wellesley. As Lisbon was still in British hands Wellesley was able to land his force in a properly equipped port instead of over an open beach. Disembarkation began on 22 April 1809.

The struggle that now ensued was between two very different armies. The British were able to import by sea the greater part of their requirements while those that they obtained locally were promptly paid for by the commissariat staff. This was not a simple matter. The army was always short of money and requests to the British government for further supplies recur time and again in Wellesley's correspondence. To quote two examples. In March 1810 he wrote to the Prime Minister that 'the whole system of the discipline, efficiency and equipment of the British army depends on regular payments.' Again in July 1812 he stated quite bluntly 'war cannot be carried on without money.' Towards the end of the war in the south of France he was reduced to having French pieces coined so that he could pay the troops.

He was also a strict disciplinarian with a marked respect for the local people, their property and religion. Any interference with the inhabitants by his soldiers was severely punished. Moreover, he was extremely tactful in his dealings with the Portuguese and Spanish authorities. As a result the men of his army became almost universally popular and fraternization was general. This happy state of affairs continued even when the army crossed into France where the local villagers much preferred the British to their own soldiers. The behaviour of the French was very different. It was their custom to live off the resources of any country which they happened to be occupying and to take what they wanted by force. Any resistance was treated with great brutality. The local inhabitants were naturally only too ready to take their revenge whenever opportunity offered. Isolated French soldiers and even small parties ran the risk of being ambushed and murdered, often by somewhat barbaric methods. Couriers carrying important messages had to be accompanied by strong escorts. In later life the Duke of Wellington, as he had then become, explained to Earl Stanhope the advantages of his system: 'I made a computation of all the men I lost in Spain – killed, prisoners, deserters, everything – it amounted to 36,000 in six years. It would have been infinitely greater, but for the attention to regular subsistence. The French armies were made to take their chance and to live as they could, and their loss of men was immense.'[1] Not only did they lose men, they were forced to maintain fortified garrisons throughout the country and the consequent dispersal of their troops was an important factor in enabling Wellesley, whose total manpower in the Peninsula was often outnumbered by ten to one, to bring the French to battle on reasonably equal terms. It should be added that the Portuguese army, after a period of training under British officers, eventually became formidable soldiers who fought bravely and were highly regarded by Wellington. Though the Spanish army was of little use, their guerrillas were of great value and provided considerable assistance to the British throughout the war.

When disembarkation was complete Wellesley wasted no time lingering in Lisbon. He quickly marched north to deal with Marshal Soult who had reoccupied northern Portugal. On 12 May

1809 he crossed the River Douro and defeated Soult – one of Napoleon's most able generals – who was forced to evacuate the country through the northern passes with great loss of men and material. Wellesley then turned south with the intention of marching on Madrid in collaboration with a Spanish army commanded by General Cuesta. The Spanish proved to be more of a liability than an asset and did little to assist the British in the battle of Talavera, where Marshal Victor, whose troops outnumbered the British by two to one, was defeated on 27-8 July. This victory could not be exploited because the British troops were very short of food, the Spaniards having failed to produce the supplies they had promised. In addition, powerful reinforcements were known to be marching to the assistance of the vanquished Marshal Victor. Wellesley, therefore, withdrew at once into Portugal. As a reward for his success at Talavera he was created Viscount Wellington.

In the meantime, Napoleon had won a decisive victory over the Austrian army at Wagram which forced the Austrians to sue for peace. It was clear to Wellington that the consequent release of French troops would result in Napoleon's sending reinforcements to the Peninsula. He now began his patient, long-sighted strategy which, after a further five years' hard struggle, would end with the expulsion of the French from Spain and the allied advance into France. The first step was the formation of a firm base from which the British could not be dislodged and into which ships could deliver supplies without hindrance. Lisbon was the chosen base and, to protect it, in the winter of 1809-10 construction was begun on the famous triple Lines of Torres Vedras.

As Wellington had foreseen, the summer of 1810 saw the arrival of substantial French reinforcements in the Peninsula, bringing their total strength in Spain up to 350,000. Of these Marshal Masséna, considered by Wellington to be the ablest of the French marshals, was to command 100,000 experienced troops. His orders were to drive the British into the sea. His first move was to capture Ciudad Rodrigo, the Spanish fortress which guarded the north-eastern strategic road from Spain into Portugal. This was accomplished by Ney, his second-in-command, on 10 July. Much bad feeling was caused by Wellington's refusal to make any attempt to save the fortress, but at this stage in his operations it was no part of his long-term plan to risk any section of his all-too-small army.

After the fall of Ciudad Rodrigo Masséna commenced his advance into Portugal. Wellington fell back before him, laying waste the country as he retired and shepherding many of the inhabitants back into the safety of the Lisbon defences, while urging others to take refuge in the mountains. In the course of his retreat he occupied an impregnable position on the heights of Busaco. Masséna, over-confident of success and preoccupied with the attractive Madame Heberton who had accompanied him to the war, failed to carry out a proper reconnaissance, and his subsequent attack on 27 September was beaten back with considerable loss to himself and negligible damage to the defenders. This battle was fought by Wellington more for political than strategic reasons, its purpose being to raise the morale of the British people who, without a victory, might have become depressed at the news of their army's again retiring to a possible port of evacuation.

After the battle the British withdrew to their prepared lines. When Masséna came face to face with these he was aghast at their strength. He was not prepared to risk a second Busaco by attacking such a strong position which was covered by 600 guns and defended by 30,000 British troops, supported by a large contingent of Portuguese. He stood his ground for four months during which he lost 20,000 men, mostly from hunger and disease in the devastated countryside. While the French suffered, the British were enjoying good and plentiful food. The officers, when not on duty, were able to shoot, fish and organize race meetings. The men played games and danced with the girls. Some lucky souls even managed a spell of home leave.

By the beginning of March 1811 Masséna realized that if his army was not to be destroyed he must evacuate Portugal. His retreat, though well conducted, was continually harassed by the British advanced guards. By April the British army was back on the Spanish frontier. Masséna made one last effort to relieve his garrison in the Portuguese frontier fortress of Almeida but was repulsed at the battle of Fuentes d'Oñoro. The French never entered Portugal again. March 1811 also saw the victory of the British garrison of Cadiz over the French at the battle of Barrosa.

This was the moment for the second step in Wellington's progressive strategy for the recovery of the Peninsula. In the first stage he had operated from the firm base of Torres Vedras; now

Portugal itself was to form the base for further operations. There were two main routes from Spain into Portugal capable of carrying the impedimenta and artillery of any sizeable army. These roads were guarded on the Portuguese side of the border by the forts at Almeida and Elvas, which were already in British hands, and in Spain by Ciudad Rodrigo and Badajoz. To make Portugal secure Wellington had to hold all four strong points. He captured Ciudad Rodrigo on 19 January and Badajoz on 6 April 1812. In both fortresses, but particularly in Badajoz, the discipline of the troops broke down. Disgraceful scenes of drunkenness, robbery and rape followed the entry into these towns.

With his hold on Portugal secure, Wellington was able to embark on the liberation of Spain. He was fortunate that at this moment Napoleon had withdrawn large numbers of seasoned troops from the Peninsula for the invasion of Russia. In 1812 Wellington moved forward and won the battle of Salamanca in which he defeated Marshal Marmont and 40,000 Frenchmen in forty minutes. This was followed by his entry into Madrid and an unsuccessful attempt to take Burgos. As these operations proceeded the French, fearing for their communications with France, withdrew from Andalusia and the south of Spain. Soult, who was in command of that region, marched to Valencia to join forces with the army under Suchet. With the reinforcements he was then able to muster he advanced towards Madrid. At the same time General Clausel, who had managed to rally the army defeated at Salamanca, directed it against Burgos. Wellington was then faced by a numerically very superior enemy which forced him to fall back once more towards Portugal and his firm base.

This reverse movement, in spite of the fact that the campaign had cleared the French permanently from the south of Spain, led to much criticism from the parliamentary opposition in England where it was not yet realized that the turning point of the war had been passed. The French armies, though they still totalled over a quarter of a million, had been forced to relinquish a great part of the country. From now on they were on the retreat.

During the winter of 1812-13, while Wellington planned his next thrust, which was to expel the French from the Peninsula, the army relaxed. During the day the officers hunted with foxhounds imported from England, coursed, shot, and fished. At night there were amateur theatricals and dances, sometimes of a very elaborate nature. The men engaged in rabbiting, wrestling and village fun and games.

The year 1813 was to complete the English liberation of Spain. This was accomplished by the advance to and battle of Vitoria. The conception and execution of this campaign must rank as one of the most brilliant in military history. This was just as well, for after so many years' hard fighting everyone both at home and abroad looked for and expected the defeat of the enemy. The battle of Vitoria on 21 June drove the French out of Spain with the exception of Suchet's detachment on the east coast, which took no further part in the war.

With the French expelled from Spain, Wellington continued his long-term policy of working from a firm base. He advanced to a position in the Pyrenees but would not move into France until he had possession of the frontier fortresses of San Sebastian and Pamplona. He also took advantage of the British command of the sea to move his base for landing supplies and reinforcements forward to the small port of Passages, near San Sebastian. San Sebastian was taken by storm on 31 August and saw a repetition of the horrors of Badajoz. Pamplona surrendered at the end of October by which time the blockaded garrison was near starvation. Some severe fighting in the Pyrenees followed, after which the army crossed into France and had fought its way as far as Toulouse when it received the news that Paris had fallen to the Allies and hostilities were at an end.

The fall of Paris was the epilogue to Napoleon's disastrous invasion of Russia in which he lost half a million men and tens of thousands of horses. In an effort to re-establish his reputation for invincibility, he attributed his Russian failure entirely to the icy weather and set about raising a new army. Within four months, by almost superhuman efforts, he was able to put into the field a force of a quarter of a million men with nearly 500 guns. He was less successful in replacing his lost horses and the resultant weakness in his cavalry was a significant factor in his ensuing defeat.

The Prussians, encouraged by the French losses in Russia, at once joined the Russians in the field and, when the Austrians also united with them, the numerical superiority of the Allies became ominous. Nevertheless, in 1813 the French had the better of the battles of Lutzen (2 May) and Bautzen (21 May), though their lack of cavalry prevented them from obtaining a decisive advantage. At Leipzig on 16 October the tables were turned and the Allies were able to embark on an invasion of France which, in spite of some brilliant manoeuvring, Napoleon was unable to stem. The Allies entered Paris on 31 March 1814.

Though Napoleon was still anxious to continue the struggle, France was tired of war and his marshals refused to support him. He was forced to abdicate and was despatched to the small island of Elba with the title of king, a minute army and an annual income. After a stay of only ten months he escaped from his restricted domain with a force of about 1,000 men and landed in France. The greater part of the country accepted his return with enthusiasm and he was able to reoccupy Paris without firing a shot.

Meanwhile, the representatives of the victorious Allies were gathered in Paris discussing the reconstruction of Europe. When they heard of Napoleon's escape they immediately agreed to mobilize their armies and keep them in the field until Napoleon was finally disposed of and unable ever to disturb the peace again. Faced with such impossible odds he tried to avoid a renewed conflict by offering to agree terms, but no one was prepared to accept his word or treat with him. He was therefore forced to fight and decided that it was imperative for him to strike some massive blow before the Allies could concentrate their scattered forces. The most promising course was to attack the British and Prussian forces which were already in Belgium.

Wellington arrived in Brussels on 4 April 1815 to take over command of the Anglo-Dutch army from HRH the Prince of Orange. His arrival was welcomed on all sides. Lady Capel expressed the opinion of the British civilian colony when she wrote that his name was a host in itself. The soldiers also were overjoyed; one Sergeant Wheeler told of the 'Glorious news, Nosey has got the command, won't we give them a drubbing now.'[2]

At first the atmosphere was gay rather than warlike. When Napoleon was banished to Elba, British families, unused during the war to continental travel, had flocked to Brussels. The British officers serving in the Netherlands had also brought out their wives, and some soldiers' wives had been allowed to accompany the army. During the daytime there were cricket matches and race meetings.

At night, dinners, amateur theatricals and balls were frequent amusements. The last ball, at the Duchess of Richmond's, was still in progress when the troops were marching out of the town to meet the French.

On 15 June Napoleon crossed the Sambre at Charleroi to strike at the junction point of the British and Prussian armies. On the 16th he defeated the Prussians at Ligny but was unable to dislodge the British from Quatre Bras. So that the two armies could maintain contact Blucher courageously abandoned his line of retreat through Namur and Liège and fell back on Wavre. Wellington retired to a previously reconnoitred position at Mont St Jean, with his headquarters at Waterloo.

The great battle between the two foremost military commanders of the day was fought on the 18th and resulted in the defeat of the French army – a defeat that was turned into a rout by the intervention of Blucher's Prussians.

By the end of the day, in a battlefield barely three square miles in area, lay nearly 50,000 dead and wounded men. The French military ascendancy in Europe was over. Napoleon was banished to St Helena to eke out the remaining six years of his life building up the Napoleonic legend.

'I hope to God', said Wellington, 'that I have fought my Last Battle.'[3] Happily for Europe his prayer was answered.

Chapter

TWO

GETTING TO THE WAR

At the time of the Peninsular War the lot of the army wife, even in the home stations, was very different from that of her counterpart today. There were no such things as married quarters and the husbands were left to make the best arrangements they could for their wives. This was because under the system then existing there were very few barracks in England for the men themselves. The soldiers were normally quartered in alehouses and similar accommodation. It was not until 1792 that William Pitt, realizing the shortcomings of this undesirable arrangement, decided to make a change. It might be thought that Parliament would have been anxious to support him, but our legislators have a bad record in looking after their soldiers, and so little did those of that period care about the housing and welfare of their troops that Pitt was forced to go behind their backs and broach an obscure fund to find the money with which to buy the land and pay for the erection of the new barracks.[1]

Some units disliked the idea of soldiers being married. *The Rules and Regulations for the Cavalry* (1795) state on page 74, 'Marriage must be discouraged as much as possible. Officers must explain to the men the many miseries that women are exposed to and by every sort of persuasion they must prevent them from marrying if possible.' On the other hand, another set of regimental orders of the period pointed out, 'the marriage of soldiers is a matter of benefit to a regiment, of comfort to themselves, or of misery to both, exactly in proportion as it is under good or bad regulations.'[2] Some of the more enlightened officers were also beginning to turn their attention to improving the lot of their men's wives. To help the married women, regimental officers in one unit were instructed to have their laundry and sewing distributed among the sergeants' wives. The soldiers' washing was to be carried out by the married women of their companies. The pay for this work, little as it was, was a welcome increment to the pitifully small income their husbands received (*see* Appendix K). A regimental fund was also established to assist those wives who could not work because they were sick or lying-in.[3]

Where barracks did exist and wives were admitted, they were allowed the very minimum of privacy. Sergeant Donaldson in his book *Recollections of the Eventful Life of a Soldier* has left a description of barrack-room life. He is a valuable witness as he was an intelligent and literate man. He was born in 1794 in Glasgow, where his father, who worked in a mercantile house, gave him a good education. He was fond of reading and inspired by *Robinson Crusoe* he ran off to sea at an early age and sailed to the West Indies. On his return in 1809 he enlisted in the 94th Regiment of Foot. The following year he was sent to the Peninsula where he remained till the end of the war. He was discharged as a sergeant in 1815 and became a recruiting sergeant for the East India Company. He disliked this and moved to Glasgow where he became a head clerk and wrote the *Recollections*, published in 1825. He was a man of many talents who eventually qualified as a surgeon at Glasgow University and practised in London and Paris. He tells us of how 'he slept in the berth above Sandy and his wife'[4]. Conditions in the barracks could certainly be rowdy and rough for Donaldson goes on to say that when the night came round the room was

cleared, and the forms ranged around. An old Highlander in the room had a pair of bagpipes, which, with two fifes, constituted our music, and when we were all assembled, the drinking commenced, handing it round from one to another. After a round or two, old Donald's pipes were called for, and the men commenced dancing with the women of the company. The stamping, hallooing, and the snapping of fingers which ensued, intermingled with the droning sound of the bagpipes, was completely deafening. In the confusion some of the thirsty souls took the opportunity to help themselves out of their turn, which being observed, caused a dispute; and the liquor being expended, a join of a shilling a man was proposed to 'carry on the glory'. I was again applied to, and aided by this fresh supply, they kept up the 'spree' until one o'clock in the morning. When some of them who had got drunk began to fight, the lights were knocked out, and pokers, tongs, and tin dishes were flying about in every direction. At last the affair ended by the officer of the guard sending some of them to the guard-house, and ordering the others to bed.[5]

When a regiment was sent on active service the number of wives allowed to accompany it was restricted to six for each hundred men. The remainder were given a cash allowance to return to their homes or places of settlement (*see* Appendix A). Thereafter they received no marriage allowance or rations and were left to fend for themselves. Those who were to be allowed to embark were chosen by lot. In most cases no consideration was given to such factors as whether they were pregnant or had children who would have to accompany them. This, however, was not always the practice. In the Rifle Corps it was firmly laid down that 'women who have more than two children can never be of the number to embark'.[6]

James Anton, whom we will meet more fully in a later chapter, explains, in his book *A Military Life*, the arguments for and against allowing women with children to accompany the army.

> It is generally the case in selecting women to follow the army to a foreign station, that choice is made of those without children, as they were considered more capable of performing the services that may be required of them than those encumbered with a family; this though just as regards our wants, is not so with respect to many a deserving woman, who is thus cast upon the public, or left to her own exertions, which too often fail her in the endeavour to support herself and children, while the childless woman is selected and profits from the circumstance.[7]

The women who went abroad drew rations and could make a little money washing and mending clothes.

When a regiment was under orders to embark and the time came to select the women who were to sail with it, the typical procedure was for the wives of each company to assemble in its pay-sergeant's room along with their husbands. Tickets marked 'to-go' and 'not-to-go' were then placed in a hat. When all was prepared the women were called forward one at a time in order of seniority. As each wife drew out her ticket it was only too easy for the onlookers to distinguish those who had been successful from the many who had been unlucky. Expressions of joy and relief lit up the faces of those who were to go, while tears and anguished cries were the signals of failure, particularly if the wife was young and a baby was imminent. When a popular wife drew a winning ticket nods of approval could be seen all round the room, but growls of disappointment were apt to follow the success of an old and cantankerous scold. As only such a small proportion could go, it was inevitable that the majority would be disappointed and for them the remainder of the period before embarkation was an unhappy time.

As the moment of parting grew nearer, the tension increased up to the moment of embarkation. On the day he was to sail, one young subaltern rose early and wrote that as he walked on to the parade ground through the lifting morning mist he

> beheld companies mustering in all form. Mingling in the ranks, I could likewise distinguish the dress of females; and as the noise of assembling gradually subsided into the stillness of order, the half-suppressed shriek, and the half-stifled sob, became more and more audible. There are not many scenes in human life more striking or more harrowing to the feelings of him who regards it for the first time than the departure of a regiment upon foreign service.[8]

John Donaldson observed one young couple who, on their last night together,

> never went to bed, but sat the whole night on their berth, with their only child between them, alternately embracing it and each other, and lamenting their cruel fortune. I never witnessed in my life a more affecting scene. The poor fellow tried to assume some firmness but in vain: some feeling expression from her would throw him off his guard, and at last his grief became quite uncontrollable. When the first bugle sounded, he got up and prepared his things. Here a new source of grief sprang up. In laying aside the articles which he intended to leave, and which they had used together, the idea seemed fixed in her mind that they would never use them in that way again; and as she put

them aside, she watered them with her tears. Her tea-pot, her cups, and everything they had used in common – all had the apostrophe of sorrow. He tried to persuade her to remain in the barracks, as we had six miles to travel to the place of embarkation; but she said she would take the last moment of his company she could.[9]

When the regiments finally marched out of barracks for the quayside they were generally accompanied by the majority of the 'not-to-go' wives. This practice led to many distressing scenes as the men embarked. Officers were begged and implored to allow wives who had been unsuccessful in the draw to go aboard. But, however affected they may have been by the tears of the unhappy women, they had strict orders which were very seldom breached.

Perhaps the saddest parting of all is related by Gleig, a subaltern in the 85th Foot and later chaplain-general of the forces, in his delightful autobiography, *The Subaltern*. He tells of Duncan Stewart, a young Highlander, the son of a well-to-do farmer who made a large part of his income from smuggling. The local excise officer, whose name was Young, was not unaware of these illegal activities and had on a number of occasions managed to seize large amounts of illicit spirits from Duncan's father. There was little love lost between the two.

Under these circumstances an awkward situation arose when Duncan fell in love with Young's attractive daughter Mary. Old Stewart would not hear of any friendship with the Young family and ordered Duncan to keep away from Mary. For some time Duncan pretended to obey his father but, when he discovered that Mary was going to have his child, he married her secretly. He said nothing to his father until the arrival of the baby was imminent and it was plain that he could conceal the marriage no longer. At that time he had to take a flock of sheep to the local fair. While he was there he fortified his courage with several tots of whisky, after which he wrote to his father to tell him what he had done. At the same time a recruiting party happened to be in the inn and the leader, seeing a fine prospective recruit, plied him with further spirits until in a state of semi-intoxication he was induced to accept the King's shilling, whereupon he was whisked off to Edinburgh with a party of recruits. From there he was sent to Hythe to join a draft of the 85th Foot which was about to be sent to the Peninsula. He was given permission to send for his wife, who in her advanced stage of pregnancy made the long journey from Scotland alone. She arrived just a week before the draft was due to embark. Mary's joy at her reunion with her husband was short-lived. Just after she arrived the lots were drawn as to which women were to go abroad. Mary drew a 'not-to-go'.

On the morning the draft was due to move Mary was so distraught that some of the depot wives tried to keep her in barracks and comfort her. Despite their efforts, when she heard the column start to move she broke out, screaming that she would not be left behind. So great was her distress that permission was given for her to accompany the men to Dover where the draft was to embark. This proved to be a mistaken kindness for the column had gone only about three miles when the baby began to arrive. Duncan and his friend McIntyre were then allowed to fall out and conduct Mary to a wayside cottage where she could be cared for, on condition that they rejoined at Dover by nightfall. In the evening an officer who had been much affected by these melancholy happenings walked back down the road to meet Duncan and McIntyre. They brought the tragic news that Mary had died within a few minutes of reaching the cottage and that the child was also dead.

Duncan was given the chance to stay in England until his wife was buried but, on receiving the assurance of the depot commander that the funeral would be properly conducted, he decided that he would prefer to sail with his comrades. His spirits never recovered from the blow, he seldom spoke and was one of the first to be killed when his regiment went into action.[10]

Some wives were separated from their husbands for years. Such was the case with William Surtees, the son of a respectable Northumberland tradesman and a very religious mother. In his early years he disappointed his parents by his wild and dissolute behaviour but, when he enlisted in 1798 at the age of seventeen, he became a model soldier. He was quickly promoted to sergeant and eventually rose from the ranks to become quartermaster of his regiment, the 95th Foot. He managed to spend only two of the eight years of his married life with his wife. He was married towards the end of 1807. A few months later his battalion, which was stationed at Hythe, was ordered to Spain as part of the force which, under Sir David Baird, was to reinforce Sir John Moore's ill-fated army. When the regiment sailed on 10 September 1808, he had to leave his young wife, who was in an advanced stage of pregnancy, to make her way alone and unprotected in a series of coaches from Kent to Northumberland, where her family lived. After the disastrous retreat to Corunna in 1809, Surtees found himself back in Hythe the following February. He was rejoined there by his wife but it was not for long. In June 1810 he was again off to Spain and once more she had to rejoin her parents. On this occasion he was able to accompany her as far as London, which helped to make her long journey a little more tolerable and less lonely. The couple were not to be reunited again until 1816 when Surtees, who had returned to England and been given leave, found her looking ill and frail, probably from a tubercular infection in her chest. While he was on leave his battalion was ordered to Ireland. An uncomfortable journey proved more than the poor woman could bear and she died three days after they arrived in Dublin.[11]

Sergeant Donaldson's friend Sandy also had to leave his wife behind. When the moment to embark arrived she fell on her knees in despair before the commanding officer, beseeching him not to part her from her husband. The colonel was much affected by her distress but explained that his orders were peremptory and that she and many others like her had had as fair a chance of going as those who had been successful. She was not to be comforted; she told Sandy as he kissed her and the baby farewell that he would never see them in this world again. Her words were prophetic. Sandy was killed in a breach at Ciudad Rodrigo.[12]

Fluellyn Comyn was a band master and a bad hat. He went to the war without his wife with the most unfortunate results. Not long after arriving in Spain he made a violent attack on one of his bandsmen. Fearing that he might be punished with a sound thrashing, he deserted to the French army, where he was well received and enrolled in one of their bands. His conduct, however, showed no improvement under his new employers. It was not long before he was again in trouble with the authorities, whereupon he decided to return to the British lines. He was immediately arrested, tried by court-martial for desertion and sentenced to be shot. A reprieve by Wellington saved him from death, but he was discharged from the army with ignominy. Before he could get back to England news of the court-martial sentence reached his wife who, believing him dead, had lost very little time in acquiring a second husband. When he eventually reached home he was appalled to find that his wife was not only remarried but that she had presented his successor with a baby. After some altercation Fluellyn was able to establish his prior claim and recovered his spouse. He then re-enlisted illegally. Although his musical talent at first stood him in good stead and enabled him again to become a bandmaster, he was unable to behave decently and was again discharged as 'too bad for anything'. After this his career was lost to view though it is probable he came to a bad end. Whether his wife had any further matrimonial success is also unrecorded.[13]

Those women who were allowed to go to the wars soon discovered that life at sea had its inconveniences. The conditions on the troopships were very bad and, if the voyage was of any length, there was inevitably a good deal of sickness and ill-health. John Shipp, a drummer boy, who obtained a commission in the 87th Foot when he was still only twenty, has described how the vessel in which he sailed for India at this period was fitted with fixed beds three tiers high, between which hammocks were slung. Soldiers, their wives and children were all herded together. Many were seasick and, as the ventilation was woefully inadequate, the stench was appalling. There was a shortage of water for cleaning the decks and the situation was made even more unbearable by the groans of the sick and the howls of the children.[14] The officers were indignant about the disgraceful conditions under which the troops had to travel. Edward Paget, who became one of Wellington's generals, wrote to his father on the subject, saying, 'Can you imagine anything more thoroughly disgusting than the transportation of the finest and best troops in England . . . in ships that nothing but the basest corruption could ever have tempted men to hire into our service?'[15]

The average length of the voyage to the Peninsula was about three weeks. When the men embarked they were issued with one blanket apiece. A mattress was provided for every two men. On board the transports the sleeping areas between decks were so arranged that a space the size of a blanket was shared by six men.

The same amount of deck space had to suffice for three married couples. The berths thus allotted were arranged along the sides of the vessel and the men and their wives slept with their heads to the outside and their feet to the centre. If the ship was sufficiently wide further spaces were allotted in the centre of the deck. Boards were placed along the feet of the berths to prevent the occupants from slipping when the vessel rolled. There were no separating partitions and neither man nor woman had any privacy whatever. Donaldson says that

> stowed like any other part of a cargo, with only eighteen inches allowed for each man to lie on, we had scarcely room to move. The most of the men were seasick, and it was almost impossible to be below without becoming so. The women particularly suffered much; being crammed in indiscriminately amongst the men, and no arrangement being made for their comfort.[16]

The soldiers and their families were divided into three watches, each of which had to go on deck in rotation and remain there for four hours to reduce the congestion in the berths. Though both men and women revelled in the fresh air during their spells on deck, taking exercise could be a precarious operation if the ship was rolling or pitching. The decks were not always as clean as they should have been and became very slippery when cooks' slush and other greasy material accumulated on them.[17]

One anonymous Highlander, who sailed from Cork in 1808, reported that at one time, because of sickness, only twelve out of 250 troops on board his transport were on their feet. He proudly relates that he was one of them. He certainly had an iron constitution for he goes on to say that 'the mess I belonged to consisted of six men, but as they were all sick except myself, the whole of the provisions and rum fell to my share; and the value of this was considerably enhanced on account of its being pudding day.'[18]

The consumption of six men's rations sounds a formidable feat, even though the rations were far from plentiful. The unfortunate women were only allowed half rations. This was not nearly enough and many of them expected their husbands to lump their joint allowance together and share equally. The men were not always as generous in this matter as their wives would have liked. Disputes over the family food led to many a noisy quarrel and even the exchange of blows was not unknown.[19]

However, life on board was not all bad. There were many calm sunny days on which theatricals were arranged, the fiddle and fife were brought out, and there was singing and dancing. In one ship the men and wives were entertained by Corporal Plunkett, who danced hornpipes on the quarterdeck to the music of the regimental band. The last days of the voyage were fully occupied, the wives doing their final bits of laundry and darning while 'everyone was busily engaged in cleaning himself from the dirt inseparable from a crowded transport.'[20]

At length the ship arrived at its destination.

It is always exciting to go ashore after a period at sea, and the prospect of doing so must have been particularly exhilarating after an uncomfortable voyage in a crowded transport under war conditions. Once the army had captured the port of Lisbon the process of getting ashore was fairly straightforward. The new arrivals could stand on deck and admire the cathedrals and white houses, the flowers and the orange groves which adorned this new and exciting land. Even the boats which were to ferry them ashore were full of interest, manned by sunburned oarsmen in white clothes with red sashes.

The contingents that arrived before the occupation of Lisbon had a less spectacular but more exciting landing. They had to be taken ashore on to open beaches, often in heavy Atlantic surf. It was a common sight to see a boat overturned and its occupants thrown into the sea, very likely to be drowned. On the other hand, once these dangers had been overcome, those that got safely ashore had plenty to amuse and interest them. The local population, in colourful clothes, carrying gaily striped umbrellas, swarmed down to the beach to cheer the troops as they landed and to present them with baskets of fruit and bundles of flowers. Such a friendly welcome did much to raise the spirits of the men and women arriving in a new and unknown country. The wives were perhaps not quite so enthusiastic when they noticed the sidelong glances their spouses were getting from the sparkling eyes of the dark-haired local belles. They had, however, little time to meditate on such matters. In Wellington's army the orders for disembarkation were meticulous in their detail and in the shortest possible time after landing the columns would be forming up for a quick move to their billets or bivouac or even, if the situation demanded it, to march at once towards the enemy.

THREE

ON THE LINE OF MARCH

THE wives' troubles were by no means over after they landed. There was a nagging element of uncertainty as to whether, having endured all the discomforts of the voyage, they would be allowed to move forward with their husbands. Occasionally they had to be left behind at the place of disembarkation. In 1800, when General Abercromby's expedition sailed on its abortive attack on Cadiz, the families were all left in Minorca.[1] Eight years later, when the army was about to leave Lisbon for the campaign that led to Corunna, Sir John Moore wanted to leave the families in Portugal. Unfortunately he was not sufficiently determined and would not issue a prohibitory order. Instead he contented himself with efforts to persuade the ladies to stay behind. These suggestions were not popular and met with no response. As a result the families were allowed to march with the army and suffered appallingly in the eventual retreat.

During the Waterloo campaign, when the 42nd Royal Highlanders sailed from Ireland to Ostend, they were allowed to take four women with each company. When they disembarked the wives received the unwelcome news that only half of them would be allowed to go forward from the port. Those who were left behind were to be quartered in barracks in Ostend under the charge of a guard. When the regiment left for Ghent in barges it 'moved slowly up the canal and left the poor women behind to form their future plans for following the fortunes of their husbands'.[2] The women's arrangements appear to have been most effective and to have taken full advantage of the slackness of their guards. Two days after the regiment arrived in Ghent the abandoned wives surprised their husbands by suddenly appearing. The euphoria that followed this exploit did not last long. The escapees were quickly rounded up

26

and returned to Ostend where they were placed under a more vigilant watch. However, they were a determined bunch and after a week or two they again managed to give their guards the slip and rejoin their husbands. Impressed by their perseverance, authority decided to turn a blind eye to their misdeeds and they were allowed to accompany the regiment for the remainder of the campaign.

Normally the women who succeeded in going abroad were allowed to move forward with the army. It did not take them long to realize that the life of a campaigner was not an easy one. In the Peninsula the sun was fierce, the roads were dusty, there was little shade and the marches were often long. The children had to be attended to, the babies had to be fed. Many of the women found it difficult to keep up with the column. For this reason, soon after landing most soldiers' wives managed to acquire a small local donkey. These animals cost about four pounds, a not inconsiderable sum when it had to be found from a soldier's low pay or from any small stock of money that he might have brought out from home. Even on the donkeys the women sometimes found it hard going, for often their over-burdened animals were too slow to keep up with the marching troops. Some women fell behind when they strayed from the ranks to visit shops in the villages along the route where they could buy bread, wine and other tit-bits to supplement their rations. This habit of buying bread could be a serious embarrassment to the commissariat staff, who occasionally discovered that the women had bought the very bread which they had earmarked for the troops. It eventually became necessary to control the places where the women could be allowed to make purchases (see Appendix B). An even more reprehensible practice was that of plundering vegetable gardens. Both men and women, particularly the Portuguese ladies, were guilty, and again a strict General Order had to be issued (see Appendix G).

At the end of a day's march sleeping quarters had to be allotted and for this there was a regular drill. If the night was to be spent in a town or large village, an officer of the quartermaster-general's department went ahead of the column to make arrangements with the local authorities for billeting the trooops. This officer then allotted sections of the town to the incoming formations and these sections were then sub-allotted to battalions, whose representatives chalked on the doors of the houses signs showing which buildings were to be occupied by officers and which were assigned to each company. The number of men to be accommodated in each building was also indicated. Though the women and children had no specific right to accommodation in billets, they were fitted in whenever it was possible. (*see* Appendix H). This, however, could not always be managed. Wheatley, an English officer in the King's German Legion, kept a diary while he was on active service in which he tells of 'a miserable barn near Fuenterrabia. The family consists of one peasant about forty, two elderly, half-starved women (his wife and sister) and an Irishwoman of an English regiment who lives here because she cannot live anywhere else. Her room is a loft to which she ascends by a ladder.'[3]

When the night was to be spent in bivouacs in the country the procedure for their occupation was much the same. In this case the general himself selected an area that was suitable from a tactical point of view. When this had been done the officers of the quartermaster-general's department were soon at work apportioning areas to the battalions, the hospitals, the artillery and the commissariat magazines. If the bivouac was to be tented, the tent mules, which always led the baggage column, were brought on to the site where the tents were to be unloaded and pitched. The army became so well trained in these proceedings that the whole operation could be carried out in a remarkably short time. Private Wheeler of 51st Foot, in one of the letters which he sent home regularly during his time at the war, has left a splendid picture of the army encamping on the plains of Miranda:

I know of nothing more surprising to the eye of a stranger than to see our canvas towns rise in a moment. Indeed I was not aware myself of the effect it has on the mind until one day I was at some distance from our camp talking to some Spaniards that inhabited a small village near us. We were in full view of our division but the tents were not pitched. I heard the bugles sound to stand by the tents. I managed to draw the people's attention into an opposite direction from the camp till the bugle sounded again, this was in about a minute. I then pointed to the camp; how were they surprised. A minute before nothing was to be seen but the soldiers, now the whole camp was studded with several hundred bell tents as white as snow and as regularly placed as if it had been a work of much labour and time.[4]

It was not, of course, always quite as simple and precise as that, as John Kincaid pointed out. The son of a Scots laird, he transferred from the militia to the 95th (Rifle Brigade) in 1809 and had an exciting war. Besides being one of the storming party at Ciudad Rodrigo, he had his horse killed under him at Waterloo. He also had a pronounced sense of humour and published two entertaining books about his war experiences. He tells us that there were several

degrees of comfort to be reckoned in a bivouac, two of which will suffice. The first, and worst, is to arrive at the end of a cold wet day, too dark to see your ground, and too near the enemy to be permitted to unpack the knapsacks or to take off accoutrements; where, unencumbered with baggage or eatables of any kind, you have the consolation of knowing that things are now at their worst, and that any change must be for the better . . . You then damn the enemy for being so near you, though probably it was you that came so near to them . . . The next and most common one [as in Wheeler's description] is, when you are not required to look quite so sharp, and when the light baggage and provisions come in at the heel of the regiment.[5]

When the army had no tents, as was the case until fairly late in the war, huts had to be erected instead. To do this the men were divided into squads: some to cut branches, some to carry the logs to the lines and others to construct the huts. This business took longer than putting up tents, but it was a chore that the men much enjoyed and there was a good deal of friendly rivalry to see which company should be the first to finish and which to build the best huts. Major Moyle Sherer, of the 48th Regiment of Foot (Northamptonshire Regiment), who had considerable literary ability and in later life wrote books on Italy, Egypt and India in addition to his *Recollections of the Peninsula*, has left an attractive picture of a hutted bivouac near Castel Branco:

Our bivouac here was a delightful one: the trees were large and beautiful; a most transparent brook of sweet water ran past our lines; and the men were hutted with great comfort, and regularity. Our general occupied a small chapel by the roadside, the only building near us; and the peasants from the distance of two or three leagues, hearing that our discipline was very strict, and that we paid liberally for everything, soon established a market

29

in our camp, and brought us constant supplies of bread, milk, eggs, poultry, honey, and excellent country wine.[6]

While the preparations for establishing the bivouac were going on, some of the wives might wander off to nearby farms to try to purchase little extra luxuries. It was not often that a market such as Sherer describes was established within the camp itself. When they had made their purchases and their husbands had drawn their rations, the women set about the business of cooking the meal. This had to be done on improvised fireplaces which were generally roughly constructed of large stones. After the meals, which for the most part consisted of warm if primitive stews, had been consumed there was plenty of laundry and darning to be done. Here the women were in great demand and many bachelors had to fend for themselves. Donaldson tells us that it was at the war 'I first learned to wash my own clothes. I was awkward enough when I began, but practice soon made me expert at it.'[7]

After a time, as the work was finished, small parties of men and women would gather together and stretch their weary limbs on the hard ground. The rum ration would be passed round, pipes lit up and tales exchanged about the events of the day. Eventually all except the sentries would turn in for a night's sleep. This was not always uninterrupted. The country was infested with large green lizards and other vermin such as spiders, mosquitoes, scorpions, snakes, ants and flies which often managed to insinuate themselves into blankets and clothes, making life very uncomfortable. There was also a danger of sparks flying from the numerous camp fires, and serious conflagrations were not unknown. In one fire the 23rd Light Dragoons lost over a hundred saddles.

In addition to the inevitable hardships of such a life, both in camp and on the line of march, there was often an element of danger from enemy action. This was particularly so when the army was retreating. At such times morale tended to be low and discipline lax. Some of the wives were as badly behaved and drank as hard as the men. At Bembibre, during the retreat to Corunna, the wine stores were pillaged and dreadful scenes of drunkenness ensued. Groups of soldiers, women and even children were to be seen lying in the streets, 'Inanimate, except when here and there a leg or arm was seen to move, while the wine oozing from their lips and nostrils seemed the effect of gunshot wounds.'[8] Strenuous efforts were made to get these drunken wretches to their feet so that they could continue the march. Some were persuaded to make the effort but others, who had to be left behind, were later ridden down by the pursuing French cavalry. Men and women were crushed under the horses' hooves or slashed to pieces by the riders' sabres.

Wellington himself had no illusions about what to expect from the more hardened of the females. In later years he expressed the view that the women were every bit as bad as the men, if not worse, when it came to plundering.[9] His great opponent, Napoleon, was of the same opinion, 'Women when they are bad,' said he, 'are worse than men, and more ready to commit crimes. The soft sex, when degraded, falls lower than the other. Women are always much better, or much worse than men.'[10] Certainly there were occasions when their behaviour was so bad that the provost staff had to make an example of some of the worst of them by administering a sound thrashing.* The provosts' patience must often have been severely tried in ensuring that their orders were obeyed. To enforce their directions they sometimes resorted to very harsh methods. On one occasion during the retreat from Burgos in 1812, after issuing repeated warnings to the women that they were not to get ahead of the column and block the roads, they had no compunction in shooting two of the precious donkeys belonging to wives who persisted in disobeying them. The unfortunate owners were then left to pick up and rescue as many of their belongings as they were able to carry on their backs. In spite of the rough treatment offenders received, the lack of discipline among some of the women persisted throughout the war in the Peninsula and reappeared during the Waterloo campaign. Writing of the advance into France after the great battle, Mercer, who commanded a troop of Royal Horse Artillery, related that 'when we resumed our march there was no cessation, no diminution of the crowd. The number of

* In 1850 the Austrian Marshall Haynau, who was reputed to have flogged women in the Hungarian rebellion, visited England and was mobbed by the draymen of Barclay's brewery. This was followed by charges that Wellington had flogged women in the Peninsula. He denied having any hand in such a practice but admitted that some women might have been flogged under the provost's orders. If this was so the army was no more brutal than the rest of the nation since the flogging of women in civilian gaols continued until it was abolished by George IV at the request of Lady Conyngham.

servants, suttlers, stragglers and women was incredible and added not a little to the general confusion.'[11]

If the Provosts were hard on the women who got in front of the columns and blocked the road, there were also dangers for those who lagged behind. On one occasion a surprise cavalry attack on a rearguard resulted in a number of women being taken prisoner. There were fears for their lives and their virtue. In fact, they were luckier than anyone expected. The following day the French returned all of them unharmed.[12] History does not relate whether this was because they were too much trouble to hold or whether they were not fair enough of face to please their captors. Possibly the former as, at the same period, another French cavalry raid on a baggage column captured a number of prisoners among whom, Sergeant Costello of the 95th Rifles recalled,

> were several children in panniers carried by donkeys. One Irish woman, in particular, I remember seeing, whose grief seemed inconsolable for the loss she had sustained in that of her child. In a few days, however, the French, desiring to be as little encumbered as ourselves with children, sent them back with a flag of truce.[13]

When earlier in the campaign some French women had been captured by the Spaniards at Benevente they did not receive such gallant treatment. The French garrison had been surprised during the night. Without even time to dress they sprang to arms but were temporarily driven back. During the fighting they suffered fairly severe casualties and a number were taken prisoner. Among those captured were several women, including the wife of the colonel of the 19th Regiment. The next morning the Spaniards returned the ladies but to the mortification of the French they were sent back completely naked.[14]

To be captured was bad enough but there were even worse dangers to be endured. In November 1812 the 51st Foot were posted near a bridge outside Valladolid. Sergeant Maibee was on duty at the bridge and his wife was preparing breakfast in the battalion camp so that it would be ready for him on his return. The enemy were approaching and to cover their advance they brought some guns into action. These started to shell the camp. The very first round fell as Mrs Maibee was taking some hot chocolate off the fire. It carried away her right arm and breast killing her instantly.[15]

Though those officers who wished to take their wives to the front had to make all their own arrangements, a number of them still did so. These wives shared all the dangers of the soldiers' families, but the hardships they had to suffer, though often severe, were appreciably less. Mrs Currie was a case in point. She was a pretty little woman married to an ADC to General Hill, Wellington's most trusted and most able general, who at that time was commanding the 2nd Division. On the line of march she used to accompany the 2nd Divisional staff riding on a mule, looking very attractive in a smart dress and wearing a small straw hat. She generally carried a parasol and her small dog sat on her knee. A nanny goat trotted along by the side of the mule. This served as a mobile dairy to provide milk for her small baby, who had also been brought to the war. The baby, wrapped in green silk, was carried by an Irish nurse who walked along chatting to the batman. Behind them followed a donkey led by an English liveried servant mounted on a strong and serviceable cob. The donkey was laden with the usual pile of luggage, topped by a cage of canaries. This comparative comfort was accepted as correct for a lady in Mrs Currie's position. She was a great favourite with the officers and, whenever possible, dined at the general's table, with the admirable result that the staff 'neither forgot the deference due to beauty nor the polished manners of the drawing room'.[16]*

Mr Larpent, the judge advocate-general, made a similar, though more homely observation in his diary when he recorded that 'I dine occasionally with Major and Mrs Scobell, who give very pleasant little dinners, and tender meat, and a loo party afterwards.'[17] These small touches of home life must have been more than welcome to the fighting men, many of whom did not see their families for years on end.

During the long years, as the columns marched backwards and forwards across the Peninsula, a real feeling of good-fellowship developed throughout all ranks. Anticipating Kipling, the women discovered that the colonel's lady and Judy O'Grady had very

---

* Currie, then a colonel but still ADC to General Hill, was killed late in the evening at Waterloo. He was stripped of all his clothing by marauders and his body was found only with some difficulty the morning after the battle.

much in common. As for their husbands, Sergeant Costello noticed that 'Lords found that they were men and men that they were comrades.'[18] For all of them there was plenty of excitement, great discomfort, much to laugh at and to cry about. Many of the women were as tough as the men. On the whole they probably enjoyed the life and would not have exchanged places with those who had drawn a 'not-to-go' ticket.

Chapter
FOUR

THE RECOLLECTIONS OF MARY ANTON

WAR has been described as a sequence of long periods of great boredom punctuated by moments of great fear. It is certainly true that though there were many colourful and dramatic episodes to brighten the hard life of the women who followed Wellington's army, for the most part their existence consisted of sheer hard slogging. This can be illustrated by the tale of one typical wife which may serve as a background to some of the more picturesque stories that follow later.

Mary was the wife of James Anton, who enlisted in the militia but later transferred to the regular army and eventually became Quartermaster of the 42nd Royal Highland Regiment (the Black Watch). James was the son of a village schoolmistress. His mother was a strict non-conformist and a devout woman, known for her good works. Her academic qualifications were less apparent. When James joined the militia in 1802 he claimed that he was filled with sound principles but little learning. His appearance may also have been rather below standard as, shortly after joining his regiment, he lost the opportunity of becoming an officer's servant because of his inability to clean his own shoes.

His early days in the army provided a discouraging change from his life at home. He found his new companions were considerably less high-minded than his mother, his quarters were not nearly as comfortable as his room at home, and his food was a great deal less appetizing. One Edinburgh landlady explained away the poor quality of the meals she provided by telling him that 'it takes a deal of dirt to poison soldiers'.

In 1812 he joined the 42nd Foot, a regular army unit, at Inverness. He soon attained the rank of sergeant and was sent to Edinburgh on a recruiting drive. While he was there he met an old girlfriend from his militia days and married her. It might be thought that it was his early discomforts and the bad food provided by Scottish landladies that had driven him to the altar, but this was not the case. The marriage was a real love match. He was devoted to his Mary, who accompanied him wherever he went for the remainder of his service.

The year after they were married a draft was made up to reinforce the battalion of the regiment which was serving in the Peninsula. James was included in the draft and Mary was lucky enough to draw a 'to-go' ticket. He and Mary embarked in one of the coastal vessels that were to carry the party to Gravesend. On arrival at that port they transferred to the transport in which they were to sail to Spain.

The voyage lasted three weeks. James, who was appalled at the conditions and lack of privacy that the wives were expected to endure on the ship, managed to obtain the use of one of the ship's boats as living and sleeping accommodation for himself and Mary. Each day he handed over their rum ration to the ship's cook and, in exchange, he was lent a tarpaulin to throw over the boat at night and was given hot water to make tea and coffee. During the voyage Mary employed much of her time in sewing, and managed to make a little money by repairing clothing for the unaccompanied men. She and James thought themselves very lucky to be able to travel in this way, regarding themselves as the 'most comfortable of the uncomfortable'.

It was September 1813 when they landed at Passages. Their first two nights ashore were spent in an old convent at Ranturea where conditions were, if anything, worse than they had been on the ship. James's vivid description of this unpleasant billet deserves quoting in full:

The courts and lower part of the building were taken up by batmen, muleteers, and bullock-drivers, with their horses, mules, asses and oxen. The dilapidated apartments above were assigned for the quarters of the soldiers, who found it necessary to unhinge the doors and window shutters, on purpose to cover the joists, from which the flooring had been torn up for fuel. The slabs were raised from the lobbies and courts below, and laid in the centre of the upper rooms for the purpose of fireplaces. Thus, by hasty devastations, this once revered abode of monks, friars, and priests, was exposed to every kind of pollution, blackened with the smoke of a hundred fires fed by its own altars and furniture, and the walls left a naked monument of the ravages of war. If the confusion of Babel was bad, this was worse. Below, the tinkling of mule-bells never ceased, the neighing of the horses was answered by the braying of the mules and asses; the bellowing of the half-starved oxen mingled with these, and echoed through every room and vault of the building; while the loud and frequent exclamations of *Carachue* by the muleteers, gave no rest but to such as were totally overpowered with sleep. Indeed, a number of the men were far from being disposed to rest, some having indulged themselves too freely in the juice of the grape, or the more pernicious libations of *aquadent*, heretofore unknown to them; others were disposed for singing or merriment; while loud exclamations of discontent burst from twenty mouths at once. Amidst this scene of uproar, some poor luckless wight, with disordered stomach and bowels, was scrambling on all fours, groping his passage to the door, getting a kick from one and an oath from another, till unable in the darkness to find egress, he discharged his unwelcome burden upon some one asleep.[1]

In the background the guns that were battering the walls of San Sebastian sounded a continual reminder that the end of the voyage had brought them to the war. Many a wife must have thought that the battlefield would have little worse to offer than their first billet in Spain.

The Antons were more than glad when the time came to leave these miserable surroundings. Their destination was Lezaca, which at that time was the site of Wellington's headquarters. Unfortunately, the captain who was leading their party lost his way and led them along a precipitous Pyrenean pass, where one false step might mean instant death. The country was magnificent and 'at times the eye was gratified with the most romantic views; but soldiers, almost breathless, and panting beneath the burden of arms, ammunition, accoutrements, and heavy knapsacks, felt little pleasure in feasting their eyes on such scenes of solitary grandeur.'[2]

Though James and Mary were duly thankful to arrive safely at their new home, their hearts sank when they discovered that they were to be accommodated in another convent. Conditions actually turned out to be rather better than they had been at Ranturea but, in spite of their long and perilous march, they again managed to get very little sleep. Much of the night was spent putting out a fire which had been started by a careless soldier cooking his meal on a wooden floor. The next day James's draft moved off to join their battalion which was then in the 6th Division commanded by General Clinton. The battalion had recently acquired a new colonel and Anton was disappointed to find that the discipline was not at all good and the drill below standard. His first task, however, was to find accommodation for Mary. As the battalion was in the Pyrenees the choice was bleak. It rested between lying in the open where the dew was heavy and the night air cold, or in sharing a tent with eleven other soldiers. The Antons chose the tent. The next day they determined to make other arrangements. Not only did they wish to have a little more privacy, but they had made the unpleasant discovery that the men of the battalion were all suffering from an irritating skin disease caused by the filth of their clothes, which for some time they had had no opportunity to change or remove.

James decided that his best course was to erect a small hut. The first task was to dig holes for the uprights. James relates that

> on breaking the surface of the ground, where the ends of the boughs were to be inserted, I laid open a nest of snakes, which not a little startled my poor wife, who became apprehensive, as the green turf was to be our bed, that there might be more of those reptiles under cover to do us injury; but she became somewhat reconciled to the spot, when assured that they were of a harmless kind. With the assistance of a few willing hands, I finished the hut in the course of the day, so that it served for a temporary shelter, and prevented myself and my wife depriving the men of their very limited accommodation in the tent. When I stretched myself down at night, in my new habitation, my head rested against the one end while my feet touched the other, at which was the entrance; my wife's apron being hung up as a substitute for a door, a couple of pins on each side served for lock and hinges; and feeble as that barrier was, none of the men

entered when that was suspended, and we might have left it to its own keeping, from morning till night, without an article being abstracted; thieving, indeed, was unknown in the regiment; but in fact there was little of worth to steal amongst us.[3]

Humble as this new abode may have been, it was a home of their own and by far the best accommodation they had enjoyed since leaving Scotland. Encouraged by this success, they decided when the regiment moved forward to a new site to set about erecting larger and more ambitious accommodation. This time luck was against them. Two days after the new hut was finished a flood, the result of some heavy rainfall, carried off a large part of their slender possessions, including their provisions for the next day. To add to their distress a violent gale bore away their fragile roof. They were then forced to spend the remainder of a very uncomfortable night sheltering as best they could in the lee of a mountain rock. There was no tent to creep into, not even one full of soldiers. They had all been blown down in the storm. The morning brought further troubles to add to Mary's misery. James went off to carry out his duties, leaving her to do the housekeeping. She spent rather more than they could afford on some bread and wine to replace the lost rations and then set off with her purchases to join James, who was on an advanced picquet.[*] She had only gone a little way along a steep and narrow path when her foot slipped and she fell down the slope. Fortunately she was not badly hurt and escaped with a nasty shaking and a bad fright. More seriously, in the fall she had lost her precious parcel. With great determination she returned to the camp, dipped once more into their dwindling stock of money, bought another loaf and more wine, and set off on a second attempt to reach her husband, who had gone on duty without food. This time she made the journey successfully, though by the time she had reached the picquet and was able to give her hungry husband his much needed breakfast, she had used up her final resources and sank to the ground, weeping bitterly.

James did his best to comfort her and, at the end of his tour of duty with the picquet, his first thought on returning to camp was to

[*] Picquet. Modern and perhaps better understood spelling 'picket'; a small detachment of advanced troops posted to give early warning of an enemy attack.

erect a new hut to shelter her. He had learned most of the tricks of hut building from his previous efforts and was determined that this new attempt would produce a much improved abode. For the next three days he spent the whole of his free time building their new home and, when it was finished, he and Mary agreed that it was in every way superior to many a Highland bothy or Irish cabin. Every day some improvement was made, and eventually a fireplace was installed. The young couple, delighted with this latest refinement, merrily set out to gather sticks so that they could try out this luxurious addition to their bower. When the fuel was collected they lit the fire. The chimney drew perfectly and home soon became snug and warm. But on that very night the order was passed round that the regiment was to march at first light the following morning. In the dull dawn, as she walked away and looked back at the little shelter they had worked so hard to make comfortable, it is not surprising that Mary once more dissolved in tears.

That day the regiment fought its way across the Nivelle and at night, when the women came up from the rear to join their husbands, there was no inviting hut with a warm fire to sleep in. Mary had to lie out in the open with only a blanket to cover her. Providentially, although the night was cold and frosty it remained dry. There were many worse nights to come. As the regiment advanced towards the Nive the wind and rain became progressively colder and more bitter, shoes wore out, feet were torn and sore. At one time the battalion occupied an area where the ground was so soggy that it became known as the 'wet camp'. Men and women were all relieved when a halt was called and the army ordered into cantonments.

The resulting improvement in living conditions was much appreciated and, though the men were kept busy and food was short, there was very little grumbling. Everyone recognized the appalling conditions with which the commissariat staff were trying to contend. It is characteristic of the British soldier and his wife that they will put up with any amount of hardship without complaint so long as they are confident that those in authority are doing all that they can to help them. The rations were generally made up of ship's biscuits, frequently crushed to crumbs or moulded to dust, one pound of beef and one pint of spirits, which as a rule was of excellent quality. A strange but popular breakfast was

A sad parting after drawing a 'Not-to-Go' ticket.

Wellington's army landing at Mondego Bay in 1808, with women lending a hand.

English troops and families encamped in the Bois de Boulogne, September 1815.

Scenes on the line of march: some women managed to acquire a donkey, while others travelled on baggage wagons.

composed of toasted biscuit dipped in spirits. Occasionally these rations were supplemented with a little rice though there was no entitlement to this commodity on the ration scale. Salt was almost unobtainable.

The respite was short. On 6 December 1813 the 6th Division forced a crossing of the Nive. The following night, during which there was heavy rain and a snowfall, was spent in bivouac. James and Mary slept in the open trying to keep themselves warm beside a camp fire. Uncomfortable as they were, all thoughts of their own troubles were put into the shade by their indignation at the treatment meted out to the wife of another sergeant. The husband, who was in charge of the guard, had managed to secure a small pigsty near his post to shelter his wife, 'a comely, modest, interesting young woman'. After the couple had cleaned the sty out and made it reasonably comfortable, the adjutant's clerk, who had kept out of the way during the fighting, came forward. He then asserted his position to turn the poor woman out into the open. In Anton's opinion there were many women in the regiment who would have defied this unpleasant creature and kept him at bay. This one had too gentle a nature and suffered accordingly.

As the days went by the weather became so bitter that the fighting had to stop for a second time. The troops were then put into billets. As there was a serious shortage of accommodation in front of Bayonne, the officers of the 42nd gave up a large part of the space allotted to them so that all the married personnel could be housed. This enabled every family to have one room to itself. The main worry then was the lack of fuel. Wood was very scarce and what was available was for the most part green timber which smoked a lot and gave out very little heat. This made it very difficult for Mary and the other wives to produce appetizing meals. In addition to dealing with the problems posed by cooking on the wretched fires, they had to contend with meat of poor quality, no vegetables and very little rice. In these trying conditions the commissariat butchers soon discovered that they could make a substantial increment to their pay by selling the wives the blood and offal of the slaughtered cattle. Any food bought from the local population was prohibitively expensive.

We were paying at this time, two shillings and sixpence for a loaf of bread, between two and three pounds weight, termed a 'Pampolonia'; the same price was asked for a pound of brown sugar; a pound of soap was the same price; and an English pint of milk was tenpence, but that could rarely be obtained. Coffee and tea were scarce articles, and beyond the price of a soldier's purse.[4]

The regiment remained in its cantonments until February. When the order to move arrived, James was away on picquet duty, and Mary was left to pack up their belongings on her own. As bad luck would have it she was doing her laundry when the orders came. This meant that she had to bundle up their linen while it was still wet and heavy. At the time she was without a donkey and therefore had to make her way forwards, carrying the family belongings on her own back. At the end of the day's march, as she was not to be found with the column, James was given permission to go back and look for her. After about an hour's walk he came upon her sitting exhausted and miserable by the side of the road. Worn out and quite unable to carry her burden any further, she was overjoyed to see her husband approaching. It did not take her long to recover her spirits and, in a short time, they were happily on their way to camp with their household goods on James' broader shoulders.

At the crossing of the Adour another sergeant's wife was not so lucky. This unfortunate woman was crossing the river on a small donkey with a child in her arms when the heavily laden little animal stumbled on the slippery stones which formed the river bed. In its fright the child gave a violent jump and the mother dropped it in the river. Seeing her child being swept away by the rapid current, the desperate mother leapt into the water in an attempt to save it but she was then herself swept away. When the father, who was not far away, saw what was happening, he at once rushed over and plunged in to try and rescue his family. He too was soon in difficulties. His comrades after great exertions managed to rescue him, but the mother and child were never recovered.

After this tragic event the remainder of the women were ordered to wait on the near side of the river until a bridge that had been partially destroyed by the French was repaired. Mary was one of those who had to wait. James at the time was away in front acting as orderly to General Pack, the brigade commander. While she was waiting she was approached by another wife who wanted to go back to St Severe to do some shopping. This woman asked Mary if she would look after her donkey while she was away. Mary agreed to do this. When the time came to cross the bridge, as the woman had not returned, Mary started to lead the donkey over. When they had reached the middle of the bridge the animal decided that he had gone far enough and dug in his toes refusing to move another inch. This caused a block on the narrow track and, when another regiment started to cross, Mary feared that she would have to abandon the obstinate donkey and carry forward the other woman's belongings as well as her own. This she would almost certainly have had to do had it not happened that she was carrying on her shoulder a horn engraved with the masonic arms. A passing grenadier, a fine strapping fellow, happened to notice this horn. He at once handed his musket to a friend and, picking up the small donkey in his arms, carried it to the end of the bridge. As he continued on his way to catch his companions, he smiled at Mary and said to her, 'Poor creature, I could not see you left struggling there for the sake of what is slung by your side.' Sergeant Anton makes an interesting comment on such acts of kindness:

Perhaps the reader may be desirous to know how the women following the army on an hostile campaign, such as this which I am attempting to describe, bear the hardships to which they are exposed, when thus left behind their regiments, and absent from their husbands? I may be permitted to say, that the manner in which they have to bear hardships, even with their husbands, is anything but pleasant; and would be unsupportable were it not that each sees her neighbour suffering as much as herself. Her bed is generally on a damp ground; her threadbare mantle, which envelops her bundle by day, serves for a sheet by night and her husband's blanket for a coverlet. Accustomed to such usage as this, she can scarcely meet with worse when absent. Indeed the kindly manner in which the benighted women were received at any of the corps cantoned in the houses by the way was highly creditable to the army, and sometimes rendered the wayfarers more comfortable than they would have been with their respective regiments, seeing that they had found shelter in a house.[5]

43

*   *   *

After the capture of Toulouse the 42nd were ordered to move to Auch. Mary seems to have been fated to be by herself when orders for a move arrived. On this occasion James was away from camp on duty in the town. When he returned he discovered that the regiment had moved off but that Mary was waiting for him. He found her sitting on his knapsack, a lonely and woebegone little figure. Together they set off in pursuit of the column but had still not caught up by nightfall. As night approached they were lucky to fall in with the 74th Regiment of Foot (Highlanders), who received them with great kindness and put them up for the night. The next morning the sound of the 42nd Regiment's pipes reassured them that they were not far from their friends. They were quickly on their way and soon back with the regiment.

The Peninsular War was now virtually over. With the fighting finished, much of the time at Auch was spent in dancing and other amusements, often accompanied by a good deal of insobriety. Every rank contrived to organize a ball. First the sergeants, then the corporals held their dances, and these were followed by those of the musicians, the drummers and even the officers' servants. This jollification lasted for five weeks, at the end of which the regiment was ordered to Bordeaux where it was to embark for home. The baggage was loaded on to barges and sent to the port by river. James was given charge of the 42nd's regimental barge, which formed one of a convoy under the command of Lieutenant Ford of the 79th Foot. Mary was allowed to accompany him and together they enjoyed a pleasant and restful journey, first down the River Baise with its high banks, and then along the Garonne, on the north of which vineyards, orchards and olive groves delighted the eye.

On the last evening of their journey, when the barges were approaching Bordeaux, a violent storm broke directly overhead. The helmsman of the 42nd's barge let the tiller go, the vessel ran out of control and rammed the anchor chain of a moored ship with such violence that all those who were on their feet were thrown heavily to the deck. For a short time, until the ship's crew managed to make the barge fast, there was considerable confusion and consternation on board. Most of the passengers on the barge had by this time had enough of the storm and other perils and were glad to accept an invitation to spend the night on the ship. Anton, being in charge of the regimental property, was unable to leave it and remained on the barge with the long-suffering Mary. The next morning, having handed over their responsibilities, they were able to disembark and find quarters ashore. These, after all they had gone through in the storm, seemed more than comfortable despite the absence of bed, furniture and cooking utensils.

On 21 June 1814 the regiment embarked for Ireland. Their joy at going home was great, though there were many eyes dimmed by the memory of the dead comrades they were leaving behind. Disembarking at Cork they at once marched off to Kilkenny, which was to be their peacetime station. Their stay proved to be all too short. In under a year they were re-embarking at Cork. Napoleon had escaped from Elba and they were bound for Ostend. This time only four women per company were allowed to accompany the troops but again Mary was one. On landing they went first to Ghent and then to Brussels, from where the regiment marched to fight at Quatre Bras and Waterloo. It is interesting, in parenthesis, to read that in Anton's opinion he and every soldier in Brussels at the time approved of Wellington attending the Duchess of Richmond's ball on 15 June, the night before the battle of Quatre Bras. This was criticized by his detractors at the time and more recently by Field Marshal Lord Montgomery in his book *A History of Warfare*, in which he insinuates that Wellington was unaware of what was taking place and had taken no steps to deal with the French advance, 'his army not being deployed for battle or ready to fight effectively'. In fact, the Duke was well aware of what he was about. For four days prior to the 16th he remained in the vicinity of his house so that he could be found at a moment's notice. On the 15th he issued his preliminary orders at about 5 p.m. To have cancelled the ball altogether would have been out of the question since it would have given considerable encouragement to the unreliable, Belgian anti-British element in Brussels and, at the same time, alarmed the British civilians in the city. By attending it himself he was able to keep in close touch with his senior commanders, who had also been invited, and was able to issue orders to several before he left. Anton expressed himself forcibly and at some length on the subject.

> I have heard some passing animadversions upon our great commander, for thus passing away time upon the evening of so momentous affair as that about to take place. I think as a soldier and one who was upon the spot, I have as good a right to give my opinion concerning it, as any of the croaking politicians, who were hundreds of miles from the scene of operations; and, in giving my opinion, I give it as that of every soldier who was in Brussels at the time.[6]

He goes on to give his reasons and ends by explaining how much trouble was saved by 'this fortunate ball'. Though at a distance of 150 years Montgomery sides with the 'croaking politicians, who were hundreds of miles from the scene', perhaps the men on the spot knew best.

Many of the women, including Mary, tried to follow their husbands to the battlefield. In this they were unsuccessful. Before the fighting began they 'had been forced back to the rear of the army and hurried amidst the mingled mass of fugitives, panic-stricken batmen, mules, horses, and cattle back to the gates of Brussels; but, on entering, no friendly hand stretched out to take them off the streets.'[7] This cool reception quickly changed when the news of Wellington's victory was confirmed. No 'city could boast of more hospitality than Brussels, when anxious fears for her own safety were allayed'. At long last the poor soldiers' wives, for the most part still ignorant of the fate of their husbands, were given shelter and food.

After the battle the Antons moved with the regiment into France. Their destination was Clichy, on the right bank of the Seine near Paris. Not far from their camp was a small island covered with willow trees, which provided excellent material for building huts. This pleased the Antons, who preferred living in a hut to a tent. They found it cooler in the summer and a better protection from the wind and rain in the winter. The one that James built at Clichy filled Mary with delight. It stood by the river and its small arched porch faced on to a pleasant green bank. Though it measured only eight feet by six, it was tastefully decorated with some trappings they had been lucky enough to find in a deserted house in the neighbourhood. They also managed to get hold of a comfortable small bed. Their sofa was formed from a mound of turf. A small glass window was a source of special pride.

'Twelve weeks passed pleasantly in this delightful place.'[8] Drills were short and duties light. During the remainder of the day the men were free to wander in the countryside or visit the city. At length in October, when the weather began to deteriorate, they were moved into winter quarters in St-Germain. This was only for a short time. In December they were ordered to Boulogne where they were to embark for England. Owing to some muddle the ships did not arrive at Boulogne but went to Calais. This meant one more march in cold unpleasant weather before they finally quit the continent. The voyage home, though short, was unpleasant. 'Cold blasts chill our limbs on deck, and the crowded hold emits its sickening, foul, repulsive breath.'[9]

On arrival at Ramsgate the ship collided with the pier, fortunately without serious damage. Disembarkation was carried out in a snowstorm. Two weeks were spent refitting at Chelmsford barracks after which the regiment marched home to Scotland. During the long march they were fêted as members of a victorious army deserve to be. At Cambridge the church bells were rung, the men were feasted and each woman received a present of £2. At Weatherby and Boroughbridge the men were given tobacco and the wives tea and sugar. Every town they passed through gave them a resounding welcome.

FIVE

WOMEN ON THE BATTLEFIELD

W HEN the army went into action the general rule was for the women to remain with the baggage so that they should not be involved in the fighting. Though this arrangement was really in the women's best interests, it in no way relieved, and in some cases aggravated, their anxiety about their husbands. At Sahagun, when Sir John Moore hoped that he would be able to surprise and defeat Soult, the women were left behind when the troops marched off into the night. Rifleman Harris later remembered vividly how, when the orders were countermanded and the men returned to the town, 'the wives and children of the men came rushing into the ranks, embracing the husbands and fathers they never expected to see again.'[1]

As the war went on, feelings tended to harden and Lieutenant Grattan, who served in the 88th Foot, reflected how, in January 1812, on the eve of the assault on Ciudad Rodrigo, 'those [men] who had them took leave of their wives and children – an affecting sight, but not so much as might have been expected because the women from long habit were accustomed to such scenes of danger.'[2] Gleig agreed with him. Writing about the attitude of the wives before one of Wellington's battles, he says:

On these occasions I have always been struck by the coolness of the women. You seldom hear a single expression of alarm escape them; indeed, they become, probably from habit, and from the example of others, to the full as indifferent to danger as their husbands. I fear, too, that the sort of life that they lead, after they have for any length of time followed an army in the field, sadly unsexes them (if I may be permitted to coin such a word for their benefit), at least I recollect but one instance in which any symptoms of real sorrow were shown, even by those whom the fate of battle had rendered widows.[3]

Surtees also observed how hardened women could become to the horrors of war. He noted how, after the capture of Badajoz, in April 1812,

> an officer with yellow facings came out of the town with a frail one leaning on his arm, and carrying in her other hand a cage with a bird in it; and she tripped over the bodies of the dead and dying with all the ease and indifference of a person moving in a ball-room – no more care being evinced by either of them, than if nothing extraordinary had occurred. It was really lamentable to see such an utter absence of all right feeling.[4]

Some wives refused to be left behind when their husbands went forward and contrived to leave the baggage lines to follow on to the battlefield. Others, who had initially stayed behind, could contain themselves no longer when news drifted back that their husbands had been wounded or slain. They rushed forward on foot or on their donkeys not knowing where their men might be lying or whether they would find them alive or dead.

Apart from the shock and sorrow of losing a husband, to do so at the war was a particularly serious blow to a soldier's wife. She suddenly found herself far from home, probably with little or no money, in the midst of a rough, if kindly, soldiery with no one to protect her. It was for this reason that so many remarried after the death of their husbands, some doing so two or three times during the campaign. Though many unkind remarks were made about some of the rapid remarriages, it is not difficult to understand that the poor widows had little alternative and that, even if they had no deep affection for their new mates, they were better off remarried than left alone in the midst of the soldiery. Many of the men realized this: when Rifleman Harris asked the widow of his great friend Cochan to marry him shortly after Cochan had been killed, it was largely from a sense of pity and in the hope that he could help her.[5] For the same reasons the practice of remarriage was just as prevalent in the French army as in the British. A hardened campaigner, Sergeant Burgogne, speaking of a good-looking widow, observed that 'during a campaign, if a woman is pretty she is not long without a husband'.[6] Gleig confirms this: 'Sixty women only being allowed to accompany a battalion, they are, of course, perfectly secure of obtaining as many husbands as they may choose; and hence, few widows of soldiers continue in a state of widowhood for any unreasonable time; so far, indeed, they are a highly favoured class of female society.'[7]

If a woman was unmarried she might fare even worse if her protector was killed. There was, for example, a woman who lived with a captain in the Scots Brigade. She accompanied him everywhere, sharing all his hardships and dangers. At the battle of Vitoria she remained in the approved manner with the baggage but, when she heard from a wounded soldier, who was moving to the rear, that the captain was badly hurt, she leapt on to her horse and galloped into the thick of the fray to find him and attend to his wounds. He was dead when she finally reached him and she could do no more than see that he was decently buried. She then discovered what it meant to lose a protector. We are told that she now found herself

> friendless in a strange country: . . . those who paid her any little attention in the captain's lifetime, now felt no compassion for her. Her gold watch, her favourite pony, and all that she had formerly held through her protector, were taken from her, and a short time after, I saw her struggling through the mud on the line of march with the shoes torn off her feet.[8]

In contrast to the combat areas, where the comparative shortage of prospective wives increased their desirability, they seem to have been less highly valued in more peaceful surroundings. A German, who was serving in the British army in 1814, recorded that

> In Palermo I had also the opportunity of witnessing the singular English custom of the sale of wives. A soldier of the 10th regiment of infantry sold his wife to a drummer for two pounds sterling; he, however, did not keep her long, but parted with her to the armourer of the regiment for two Spanish dollars. The woman did not appear to be at all annoyed at these dealings, but rather to be pleased with the change.[9]

There were, of course, many cases of the men showing the greatest respect to women in trouble. When Marshal Soult, in an attempt to relieve the fortress of Pamplona, attacked Wellington's army,

Dire was the consternation of the poor inhabitants when they saw us retreating through the beautiful valley of Bastan, which had been the scene of such gratulation and triumph on our advance three weeks before. Many of them, male and female, and almost all the inmates of the convents, abandoned their homes and retired with the Army. It was a painful sight to see the poor nuns quitting their convents and mixing with the troops in the dusty roads; their pale faces hectic with unwonted exertion, alarm and exposure. To the credit of our men, it ought to be told that great kindness, tenderness and inviolable respect were shown to [the ladies] on this retreat: the soldiers carried their little bundles and helped them along; and it was pleasing to observe the unsuspecting confidence with which many of these old ladies trusted themselves and their portable property to the protection of our rough grenadiers. Assuredly it was a high compliment to the character and discipline of the British army.[10]

Similarly, at the battle of Busaco in September 1810, two young women passed through the French and British lines without molestation or hindrance. One was

a poor orphan Portuguese girl, about seventeen and very handsome, [who] was seen coming from the mountain driving an ass loaded with all her property through the midst of the French army. She had abandoned her dwelling in obedience to the proclamation,* and now passed over the field of battle with childish simplicity, totally unconscious of her perilous situation and scarcely understanding which were the hostile and which the friendly troops, for no man on either side was so brutal as to molest her.[11]

The French general, Marbot, tells a similar story of how in the same battle a young and pretty mademoiselle delivered the possessions of a French senior officer, General Simon, who had been wounded and was a prisoner, through the British lines. Warned of her danger she

* Wellington had issued a proclamation that the country was to be denuded of food and people so that the French should have no means of subsistence.

went forward saying, 'we will see if the English will kill a woman'; listening to no objections she went up the hill and passed coolly between the lines of skirmishers who, savage as they were, ceased firing till she was out of range. Presently she saw the English colonel and explained what she had brought. He received her kindly and had her taken to General Simon, with whom she stayed for several days tending him to the best of her powers and leaving him only when the valet arrived. Then getting on her donkey she went through the enemy's army, by that time in retreat on Lisbon, and rejoined her regiment, without having received an insult of any kind, though she was young and very pretty. On the contrary, the English made a point of treating her with great respect.[12]

A rather different reception was accorded to a young woman near Pamplona. In 1813, when the city was surrounded by the British forces, it was known that the governor sent messages to Marshal Soult through the agency of women. To prevent these messages from getting through, an order was issued that all women passing through the British lines from the direction of the fortress were to be searched. A few days after this order had been given a young woman attempted to pass a quarter-guard carrying on her arm a basket of bread and eggs. She later said that she had hoped to sell these articles to the troops. Before she could attempt to do this she was arrested and searched, the eggs and bread being confiscated without payment. The soldiers, whose pay was at this time six months in arrears, were, in fact, literally without money and quite unable to pay for anything. When it was found that she was not carrying any messages the girl was released but she rightly insisted on complaining to the commanding officer about the treatment that she had received. She was then recompensed for the stolen goods but was refused the additional payment she demanded for loss of time and torn clothing. At this time quite a number of young women were arrested and searched somewhat unceremoniously, though no hidden despatches came to light as a result.[13]

One of those women who invariably remained as near as possible to her lover when he was in action, however dangerous it might be, was a Spanish lady who lived with Rifleman Mauley, a shoemaker in the 95th Foot. She was deeply in love with him and used to follow him into battle mounted on her donkey. The small animal was always heavily loaded as, besides herself and her belongings, it had to carry a stock of additional provisions which the enterprising lady sold to the troops, making a trifling profit to supplement her income. During the fighting in the Pyrenees, Mauley was hit in the head. His distracted companion, who as usual was nearby, on seeing what had happened left her donkey and belongings to take care of themselves and rushed over to her lover. Edward Costello, who was present at the battle, says:

> We were then in the thick of the fight, and our only safety was cover, as the balls came as thick as hail, so that every moment I expected to see the poor woman shot. She, however, seemed callous to every danger; throwing herself on the blood-stained body of her lover, she commenced giving way to the most appalling ebullition of grief, tearing her hair and wringing her hands.[14]

One of the men who was in the line was a Spaniard, who had been enlisted in the British service. He had a reputation for brutality and callousness but he now proved that, whatever his faults, he was a brave man.

> Seeing the danger his countrywoman was exposed to, he rushed boldly from his cover, and placing himself in front of her, continued loading and firing at the enemy, loudly swearing all the time such oaths as only a Spaniard can do justice to. Notwithstanding the real horrors of the scene, it was impossible to resist the impulse of laughter at the fierce grimaces and oaths of Blanco, who escaped as it were almost by a miracle.[15]

At the battle of Toulouse in 1814, the wife of Corporal Cunningham of the 42nd Foot heard that her husband had been killed. She at once hurried forward to the battlefield where some soldiers guided her to the spot where her husband was buried. They were so touched by her grief that they set to work and disinterred the body so that she might wash the wounds and see that it was decently wrapped up in a blanket. The men then replaced the corpse in the grave which was once more filled with earth. Mrs Cunningham, though bereft of her husband and with very little money, now met better treatment at the hands of fate than many other widows. An officer named McLaren, who was in her husband's company, had himself been severely wounded in the battle. When he heard of Cunningham's death he sent for the widow and employed her as his nurse. Though his wounds were too severe for him to survive, before he died he was able to make arrangements to send Mrs Cunningham home and restore her to her parents, an act of benevolence that earned him the gratitude of her family and the respect of the regiment.[16]

Nancy MacDermot was another widow who was sent home when her husband was killed. She had been a lady's maid in a nobleman's house and had married MacDermot, a pay-sergeant in the 85th Foot, against the wishes and advice of her parents. In spite of this the marriage was a great success and the young couple 'were accounted the most virtuous and happiest couple in the regiment'. MacDermot was renowned for his coolness under fire. His courage and the example he set to others, which sometimes almost amounted to foolhardiness, were to prove his undoing. One day, at the end of February 1814, during the operations outside Bayonne, the regiment was being shelled. He noticed that one or two of the young recruits were cowering down in what he considered a most unsoldierlike manner. To show them that the danger was not nearly as great as they thought, he left himself exposed on the top of a prominent sandhill. Almost at once a round shot hit his head smashing it to pieces. The news quickly got back to Nancy who at once rushed forward to the firing line. When she saw what had happened her mind gave way and she refused to believe that the mangled corpse lying on the ground was that of her husband. She had to be led back to the camp and several days went by before she could be brought to realize what had happened. An officer of the regiment writes:

At length the feeling of utter desolateness came over her; and instead of listening, as women in her situation generally listen, to the proposals of some new suitor, all her wishes pointed homewards. To her home she was accordingly sent. We raised for her a handsome subscription, every officer and man contributing something; and I have reason to believe that she is now respectably settled in Cork, though still a widow.[17]

There was a reverse side to the coin. Not all the wives behaved so well. When Private Wheeler was wounded at the battle of Nivelle, in November 1813, he just managed to crawl away into the shelter of a hedge. After some time he was found by the regimental surgeon, Dr Fitzpatrick, who dressed his wounds. He then managed to make his way to a nearby farmhouse, which had been used by the French as a commissariat stores and was therefore well supplied with liquor. When he arrived he was horrified at what he saw:

> Outside the buildings were a great many wounded soldiers, some drinking and smoking, others rolling about, some half and others mad drunk, while a great many lay stretched out as if dead. Women, too, who had followed up the rear of the army, had forgot they had come up in the laudable pursuit of seeking their husbands [and] had freely partaken of the damnable poison until they had transformed themselves into something more like fiends than angels of mercy.[18]

Nevertheless, even in the midst of this orgy there were many dutiful wives who redeemed the scene by the devoted attention they were giving to their dead and dying husbands.

> In one place you could see a lovely young woman supporting the head of her dying husband on her bosom, anxiously awaiting the last gasp for life, then again your eye would meet with one in bitter anguish, bewailing her loss, fondly clinging to the cold remains of all that was dear to her, and many more were running about mad, unconscious of where they were going or what they were doing, these had received the news of their husbands' deaths in some distant part of the field.[19]

One of these was Mrs Foster, another was Mrs Cousins, who had been widowed three times since the battle of Vitoria, which had been fought only five months earlier.

One of the most intrepid of the Peninsular wives was Mrs Susannah Dalbiac. This was the more remarkable since she had not been modelled by nature to endure the rigours of a campaigning life. She was a quiet, mild little woman, frail and delicate in appearance but was always to be found at the head of her husband's regiment, the 4th Dragoons, not only when it was on the march but quite often under fire. To sustain herself during the long marches she carried a bottle and a small haversack on the pommel of her saddle. When the army bivouacked she slept in her husband's tent, if tents were erected, but she was ready to share in every hardship and in 1811 on the Guadiana River she spent two nights in the open with the rain pouring down and nothing but a blanket to cover her.[20] On the night of 2 July 1812 the army, which was withdrawing from the River Ebro, halted in front of Salamanca. Mrs Dalbiac prepared to spend the night in the regimental lines. Ever since dusk the weather had been threatening, with occasional rumblings of thunder and flashes of lightning. At ten o'clock the storm burst. Private Wheeler saw a tree cut in two by lightning. A thunderbolt fell in the midst of the horse lines of the 5th Dragoon Guards. This caused a stampede of terrified horses. The maddened animals galloped headlong towards the Dalbiacs who were in imminent danger of being trampled to death. The colonel, with great presence of mind, seized his wife in his arms and ran with her to a nearby gun. He just had time to lay her down between the wheels before the stampede dashed past. His quick thinking undoubtedly saved them both from serious injury if not from death. The Dragoons had eighteen men badly hurt, and thirty of their horses were never recovered. The storm continued until about five in the morning.

The next day the battle of Salamanca was fought. During the fighting Dalbiac and his regiment took part in the charge of General Sir Stapleton Cotton's cavalry division, which broke the left wing of the French army and led to the capture of two thousand prisoners and a number of guns. Wellington, who was not always over-generous in his praise, rode to congratulate the cavalry in the most flattering terms. 'By God, Cotton,' he said, 'I never saw anything so beautiful in my life – the day is *yours*!' Throughout the engagement Susannah was in range of the enemy guns and was several times spattered with dust thrown up by cannon shot. In the evening, as it began to grow dark, she set off, accompanied by an orderly, to search for her husband. Somehow or other she became separated from her escort, but quite undaunted she continued her search, moving alone and unguarded through the ranks of the dead and dying. Lieutenant Tomkinson of the 16th Light Dragoons thought that no woman could have been in more unpleasant surroundings, especially when it became dark. In spite of her efforts she was unable to find her husband, who had in fact gone through the day unscathed and was still in pursuit of the enemy. Her determination did not, however, go unrewarded. During the search she came upon her cousin, Lieutenant Norcliffe, lying on the ground with a serious wound to his head. She managed to arrange for him to be carried back to Salamanca where she found a surgeon, who attended to the wound and most probably saved Norcliffe's life. In his description of the battle Sir William Napier, Peninsular soldier and historian, alluding to her exploits, comments that in addition to the bravery of the men, 'the devotion of a woman was not wanting to the illustration of this great day'.[21]

Later in the year Susannah Dalbiac took part in the retreat from Burgos during which she suffered great hardships which sapped her strength. At the end of the year she and her husband returned to England and saw no more of the war. Her excitements, though of a different kind, were not quite over; her husband became a general and she produced a daughter who married a duke.

If Mrs Dalbiac was the 'colonel's lady' of the war, Mrs Reston, the wife of a sergeant in the 94th Foot, has a good claim to be the 'Judy O'Grady'. As far as courage was concerned they were certainly sisters under the skin. During the defence of Cadiz in 1810 a small outwork known as the Matagorda was held by a weak garrison. Its defences were poor, it had no ditch around it, and it contained few bombproof shelters. As the bombproof accommodation was insufficient to house the whole garrison, the remainder had to be lodged in flimsy huts. Mrs Reston lived in one of these with her small boy. One day Matagorda was subjected to a heavy bombardment which soon blew its parapet away. Out of a garrison of one hundred and forty, sixty-four men were killed or wounded, and one of the early shots struck a hut near Mrs Reston's. Her first thought was for her child. She took him from his bed and carried him to one of the shelters. Having arranged for his safety she at once turned her hand to helping with the wounded. She sought out the overworked surgeon, to whom she rendered invaluable aid by helping him to dress the wounded men and by providing bandages, which she made by tearing up her own and her husband's linen clothing. As time passed, the water in the shelter where she was working began to run short and a young drummer-boy was ordered to go and draw some from a well that stood out in the open. The lad was obviously frightened and unwilling to leave the shelter and brave the heavy shelling. Seeing him hesitate, the surgeon told him to hurry up and not to hang about. Mrs Reston, who sensed his terror and felt sorry for him, thereupon took hold of the bucket and sallied forth herself. At first she was unlucky. As she let the bucket down into the well a shell cut the rope. Undaunted by this misfortune she collected a sailor to assist her and together they managed to retrieve the precious bucket. When it was full of the desperately needed water she carried it back to the surgeon.

When not employed in helping the surgeon, she busied herself in carrying sandbags to bolster up the damaged defences, in passing up ammunition to the guns and in carrying wine and water to the gunners. Her heroic conduct, which earned the praise of everyone in the fort, was in marked contrast to that of the only other two women in the garrison, who spent the entire period of the bombardment in hysterics.

When it was decided that Matagorda could no longer be held and must be evacuated, orders were given for the garrison to leave by boat. Mrs Reston made three crossings to the Cadiz shore, all under heavy fire, so that she could bring away not only her son but as much as she could salvage of the family possessions. Sergeant Donaldson, who was in her husband's regiment, writing in his memoirs fifteen years after these events took place, says of these crossings, 'I think I can see her yet, while the shot and shell were flying thick around her, bending her body over her son to shield him from danger by the exposure of her own person.'[22] It is sad and somewhat shaming that in addition to the tale of her bravery Sergeant Donaldson also had to record that it was 'a matter of surprise to many that the courage she displayed, and the services she rendered on that occasion should have been entirely overlooked by those who had the power of rewarding her.'[23]

The story of her later life is one of continued neglect and ingratitude. The son whom she had so bravely protected grew up and enlisted in his father's regiment. He was a most promising lad but fell foul of a bullying bandmaster. He tried to purchase his discharge but, in spite of his mother's appeals, this was not allowed. Retained in the regiment against his will, he was at length provoked into responding angrily to his tormentor's taunts. For this he was flogged for insubordination, deserted from the regiment and was never seen by his family again. When Sergeant Reston became too old to work, he and his wife had nothing but his pension of one shilling and tenpence a day to live on. As they were unable to make ends meet on this miserable pittance, Mrs Reston made an application to the military authorities for assistance. Her request was strongly supported by the officers of the regiment, who remembered her bravery at Matagorda, and received the approval of the commander-in-chief. In spite of this the secretary of state turned the application down on the grounds that he had no funds at his disposal with which to assist her. When her husband died she was removed to the Glasgow poorhouse to finish her days.[24]

In contrast, the Spaniards treated one of their heroines with the respect and appreciation she deserved. At the siege of Saragossa an artillery sergeant was accompanied by a girl named Agostina. During one of the French assaults the sergeant was killed just as he was about to fire his gun. Agostina, who was standing near him, seized the lighted match from his hand and fired the twenty-four-pounder into the head of the advancing column, which by this time was within ten paces of the gun. The effect was decisive. The head of the column was blown to pieces, the enemy recoiled and the assault was beaten off. General Palafox, who commanded the defences, was present to see this gallant act. He immediately gave the girl a sub-lieutenant's commission in the artillery and later she was granted a substantial life pension.[25]

Chapter
SIX

WOMEN IN LOVE

A S the only women allowed to accompany the troops abroad were wives, the men had no opportunity for romance with British girls unless they were widows or unfaithful spouses. In view of the uncomfortable conditions the families had to endure for long periods, it was inevitable that some of the less happy wives should look for consolation elsewhere. In such circumstances romance could quickly turn to tragedy. The story of the Battersbys is an example.

Battersby was a sergeant in the 95th Rifle Brigade. Early in 1812 he was employed as a hospital sergeant at Belem, the British base outside Lisbon. While he was leading a comparatively easy life away from the fighting, he had time to enjoy the facilities of the town and to gather with other British men and women at various social functions. In this way he met and fell in love with a married woman, who ran away with him when he left Belem to rejoin his regiment near Ciudad Rodrigo. His friends in his battalion were delighted to see him arrive with a pretty, animated English girl called Nelly, whom they assumed to be his wife. The Battersbys were a pleasant and entertaining couple and immediately became very popular in the regiment.

A short time after their arrival orders were received for a move forward to Salamanca. At the end of the first day's march the regiment bivouacked in a wood by the side of the road. At first everyone was busy working on the usual arrangements that had to be made when halting for the night. Later, when the bustle was over, dinners prepared and meals eaten, the soldiers and their wives gathered together in small groups to enjoy a brief moment of relaxation before retiring for the night. The men lit up their pipes while the women got out their needles and started to repair their husbands' badly worn uniforms. Tots of wine were passed round, tongues were loosened and the latest gossip was exchanged.

The Battersbys had joined one such group and were resting contentedly on the ground when voices were heard calling for the sergeant. As he turned to see who wanted him, a tall, well-built grenadier, wearing the uniform of the 61st Foot, appeared on the scene. The newcomer, who appeared to be under some sort of stress, walked straight over to Mrs Battersby and sat down beside her. The soldiers who were sitting near at once observed that her face became flushed and that she seemed to be very disconcerted at the sight of the new arrival. The grenadier stared at her in silence for some moments and then began to reproach her.

'Why are you leading this disgraceful and dishonourable life?' he asked her. As he spoke he was seen to flash a look of hatred and contempt towards Battersby.

Mrs Battersby, though clearly disconcerted by this attack, was by no means cowed.

'I am here,' she replied, 'because I have found someone who appreciates me more and is kinder to me than you have ever been.'

'That may be so, but have you no thought for your three-year-old child? You know that I cannot look after him and attend to all his needs. I do not want you to return to me but you must do something for the boy.'

A bitter quarrel broke out which continued for some time. The faithless wife then consented to accompany her deserted husband for part of the way back to his own camp, which lay about three miles to the rear.

Sergeant Battersby and a friend, who were disturbed by the wild looks of the grenadier, followed a little way behind the angry couple. When they had gone quite a short distance Mrs Battersby stopped and started to wish the grenadier goodnight. As she extended her hand he seized it in his own, saying as he did so,

'Are you absolutely determined to remain with your lover and desert your wretched child?'

'Yes, I am,' she said.

At this he drew his bayonet and drove it into her body, snarling, 'Well, then, take that.'

Such was the force he used to drive the bayonet home that he himself fell to the ground on top of the wounded woman. She gave one agonized scream and died immediately. The grenadier rose at once and, putting one foot on the prostrate body, tugged out the gory bayonet. Then, seeing Battersby and his friend who, being unarmed, were running back to the bivouac to summon the guard, he rushed after them intending to kill Battersby as well. He changed his mind when he saw the guard turning out. As it was obvious that his second intended victim was now safe, he gave himself up quite calmly, merely remarking, as he wiped the blood from his bayonet with his fingers, that he was sorry that his wife's seducer had not also been punished.

Nelly was buried the same evening in a shallow grave that had been dug out of the hard ground with bayonets similar to the weapon that had killed her. The grenadier was tried by court-martial. His judges took a lenient view of his crime and sentenced him to three months' solitary confinement. After serving one month of his punishment he was released and allowed to return to his regiment where he did not survive for long. He was killed in the fighting in the Pyrenees. Sergeant Battersby received no official reproach for his part in the affair. Though he survived the war in the Peninsula, he eventually suffered the same fate as his rival and died on the field of battle at Quatre Bras, on 16 June 1815.[1]

Another frail wife, the good-looking Anne Duke, was luckier in her escapades. She arrived in the Peninsula as the wife of a trooper in the 3rd Dragoons. Her hair was fair, her pink and white colouring was exquisite and she had the most beautiful blue eyes. Her attractive mouth and perfect teeth added to her charms. One admirer thought she would make the ideal model for a statue of Venus. But, besides possessing a pretty face and a shapely figure, she was ambitious and had a shrewd idea of her market value in a community where attractive women were all too rare. She quickly decided that the rough life of a trooper's wife was not for her and, as she was very quick to learn and had no difficulty in acquiring the manners and ways of a lady, it was not strange that before long her good looks and vivacity had attracted the attention of Mr Gordon, the regimental commissary. He decided that he would like to take her under his protection and the husband was pleased to make the exchange on the receipt of a substantial cash payment. Anne then became known as Mrs Gordon and lived with her new mate in Coimbra until he was transferred to the Spanish service. By this time his passion had worn a little thin and he decided that he did not wish to take his *inamorata* with him to his new post. This, however, was not such a blow to Anne as it might have been. She had learned that her lawful husband had been killed in action and that she was therefore free to marry again. This was a course she lost no time in taking and in so doing she took a further step up the seniority ladder. Her new husband was the commissary-general, with whom from then on she passed a very happy, if not always a very faithful, life.[2]

The commissaries seem to have had more time than most other people for illicit romances and one such affair in Lisbon involved two of them. Mr Larpent, the judge advocate-general, refers to them in his journal as Mr R and Mr S. These two gentlemen shared a house in which Mr R lived with an English lady, while Mr S was unattached. This arrangement worked very satisfactorily until Mr R became suspicious that Mr S was trifling with the lady's affections. He decided to question the girl, who denied that up to that time anything improper had taken place, though she confessed that she had transferred her affections to Mr S and agreed to run away with him. On hearing this Mr R pleaded with her not to desert him. He pointed out that Mr S, who had posed as his friend, had behaved in a most dishonourable fashion in making advances behind his back and that the girl would be most unwise to trust herself to such an unprincipled character. Eventually his arguments were successful. The girl agreed to renounce Mr S and remain with Mr R. Delighted at this success and thinking that he was again safely in possession of her affections, Mr R next proceeded to tackle his rival. Mr S, on being reproached for his treachery, produced a very different version of the affair. According to him it was the girl who was the betrayer. It was she who had taken the initiative and offered to be unfaithful to Mr R.

In spite of the icy atmosphere that followed these confrontations, the three of them went out together for their morning ride, followed by dinner in stony silence. All this time, although Mr R's tongue was still, his mind was in a whirl. He was at a loss to know what to do next. He was genuinely fond of the girl and appalled by Mr S's disclosures. He wondered if he could ever be happy with her again. At length, in a mood of black despair, he decided that his only course was to leave the house and sever his connection with the lady. Before departing he sought her out, told her what Mr S had said, how deeply shocked he was, and spoke of his decision to give her up. At this she burst into tears, solemnly denied the truth of Mr S's allegations and rushed off to upbraid him. A little later she and Mr S went into the garden together. Almost at once Mr R heard three pistol shots and, rushing out to see what had happened, found his mistress lying dead. As he gazed at her in horror, Mr S, holding a blood-stained handkerchief to his head, sped past him into the house. He went straight to his dressing table, took his razor from a drawer and cut his throat. A Portuguese doctor, who was the first to arrive, pronounced his wounds incurable. A more skilful English surgeon, who came hot on the heels of his local colleague, reversed this decision and managed to save his life.

At the subsequent enquiry Mr S explained that it was at the lady's request he had agreed to kill them both. Mr R declined to give the lady's name to avoid paining her connections in England. When the papers arrived in Mr Larpent's office, he had to decide whether the delinquent was to be treated as a madman or a murderer. His reaction showed more worldly wisdom than sympathy. He wrote in his journal:

> It surely was very unfortunate that the poor man had not been left in the hands of the Portuguese surgeons and doctors, who pronounced him a dead man and his wounds incurable. The skill of an English surgeon has unluckily enabled this unhappy being to stand the chance of either being hung or confined for life as a madman.[3]

Not all romances that began with difficulties ended so tragically. At Genoa in 1815 a corporal fell in love with the daughter of a non-commissioned officer in another battalion. He proposed marriage. His captain gave the necessary consent but the girl's parents would not hear of the match. He asked the chaplain what he should do and the padre sympathetically agreed to carry out the ceremony with or without the sanction of the parents. The father and mother, suspecting that some plot was afoot, kept the closest watch on their daughter. In spite of their precautions a day came when, while the father was away on parade, the corporal was able to elude the watchfulness of the mother and steal away with his beloved to the waiting parson who duly tied the nuptial knot. When the couple returned to the girl's home after the ceremony the mother tried to take her daughter away from the corporal and nearly had hysterics when she was shown the marriage certificate. By this time the men of the corporal's company had determined to celebrate the affair properly. They carried the newlyweds off to a party where the wine flowed freely, the minstrels played, and the soldiers and young women of the regiment joined together in a merry dance. Passers-by, hearing the noise, asked what festival was being celebrated. The angry parents hammered at the door but two of the men formed a guard and kept them at bay. The diarist does not relate how soon the runaways were forgiven.[4]

Those men who returned from the war on leave or to a home posting must have been an easy target for Cupid's darts. It was an old army saying that a few years in India ruined a man's eye for a horse or a woman. It is not unlikely that a period in the Peninsula had much the same effect and that those who were lucky enough to get home, were less fastidious about looks than they had been when they left for foreign lands. Many a girl with a not-so-pretty face had the war to thank for a dashing soldier as a husband. One old soldier certainly enjoyed being back among the girls. Lady Shelley, describing a visit to Althorp, wrote that, 'General Graham though in the field a hero, is in love a dotard.'[5] She was horrified at what she called his 'disgusting familiarity' with the young Lady Asgill. One can only hope that the general's success made him more indulgent to the younger officers in their flirtations.

There were, of course, many good and loving wives who endured all manner of dangers and hardships to help their wounded and battle-weary husbands. When Colonel Frazer of the Royal Horse Artillery was riding out of Lisbon he met an overburdened woman struggling along the rough road, guiding her blinded husband towards the port so that he could be shipped home to England. Along the road someone had stolen their donkey, leaving them to carry such possessions as they had on their own backs. To add to their burden their two-year-old daughter was in the arms of the sightless man while the wife carried her five-weeks-old baby, born at the war. The colonel, who was much affected by their sorry plight and the brave way in which they accepted their lot, was happy to be able to use his influence to secure them an early passage.

A certain Mrs Skiddy showed her affection for her husband in a different way. One of the most undisciplined of the wives, she had a supreme contempt for the provost staff and was prepared to risk severe punishment to secure her husband's comforts. He was batman to Lieutenant Bell of the 34th Foot and was a less robust character than his wife. On many an occasion on a long march he looked so worn out that Bell carried his musket for him. Mrs Skiddy, who knew that he needed looking after, regularly moved forward in front of the column against all regulations, saying that it was essential that she should have a fire going and the tea ready when her tired husband arrived. She also shrewdly pointed out that, if she moved in the rear of the column and was taken prisoner with her donkey, Skiddy would be quite lost and useless to the army.[6]

At the battle of Waterloo it was impossible to prevent many of the anxious women getting on to the battlefield, while the fighting was going on, to try to assist their wounded husbands. Some were hurt themselves. The wife of a sergeant of the 28th Foot was hit in two places by a shell that burst near her as she was dragging her wounded husband from the field. Mrs Eaton, the authoress of the attractive journal *Waterloo Days*, saw another poor woman, wife of a private in the 27th Foot, whose leg was dreadfully fractured by a musket ball while she was attempting to rescue her husband. He was believed to be mortally wounded but she still refused to leave him and they both had to be carried to the rear. They were eventually sent to the hospital in Antwerp where the husband survived, though the poor man lost both his arms. The wife, who was pregnant at the time, not only recovered from her wounds but later produced a healthy infant.[7]

Lastly, there is the tale of a loving wife of an officer of the 95th (Rifle Brigade). She thought of him constantly while he was absent at the war and, when he returned to England with his regiment after the miseries of the Corunna retreat, she was waiting for him on the beach. When she saw him climbing out of the ship's boat that had brought him to shore, she was unable to restrain her feelings and rushed into the sea to embrace him. Locked in each other's arms the reunited couple waded slowly to the shore. To the war-weary warrior, after all the hardships of the ghastly retreat, such a welcome must have made everything that he had endured more than worthwhile.[8]

SEVEN

A TASTE OF DULCINEAS

PRIVATE Wheeler was a philosopher as well as a soldier. During the siege of Burgos in 1812 he reflected in a letter to his mother, 'what a chequered life is a soldier's on active service. One moment seeking the bubble reputation at the cannon's mouth. The next courting some fair unknown damsel.'[1] As we have seen, the supply of British women was limited but there were plenty of Portuguese, Spanish and, later, French girls who were very ready for a little flirtation. As these were Catholic countries there was at first a slight reluctance to dally with a heretic, though this was a fear that could usually be overcome by a smooth-spoken suitor. As a last resort, since the reproach of heretic seemed to be reserved specifically for the English, the wily wooer soon learned to pass himself off as an Irishman. He was then 'considered as one of themselves, a good Christian'.[2]

Most soldiers like a pretty face and the commander-in-chief was no exception. When Wellington selected his quarters at Toulouse, it did not escape notice that the proprietress was a Spanish beauty who had married into a French family of rank. Larpent coyly observed that, though he did not wish to be scandalous, the looks of the lady 'may perhaps have decided the choice of the house'.[3]

Another senior officer who appreciated good looks was the redoubtable Sir Thomas Picton. A fine fighting general, he was adored by his troops in spite of his forbidding looks and gruff speech. He was no respecter of persons and Wellington, who admired his courage and ability, was inclined to resent what he regarded as his over-familiar manner. He could also be markedly unorthodox in his dress and in 1815, having received rather late orders to take command of the 5th Division, arrived in Ostend without his uniform. During the Waterloo campaign he was attired in a blue frock-coat, a black silk neckcloth, dark trousers, boots and a round hat. The night he arrived in Ostend he and Captain Gronow, his acting ADC, stayed at a hotel in the square, where the captain spent an amusing evening watching the general conducting a flirtation in excellent French with a good-looking waitress.[4] Under these circumstances it was inevitable that the army should collect a large number of additional female followers from the countries they passed through.

These additions to the train were not always encouraged. A Scottish soldier of the 71st Regiment of Foot (Glasgow Highlanders), has left an amusing account of his regiment's departure from Boho in 1813. The men had spent a very lively winter in this small village. There was dancing every night, including Sundays. None of the girls and few of the men had any inhibitions about Sabbath-breaking though a few of the latter were 'more scupulous on account of the day'. When the time came for the army to leave there were many broken hearts and tearful eyes. Every man tied a handkerchief on to his ramrod as a token of farewell and the whole village turned out to wave goodbye. Some of the girls could not bear to be separated from their lovers and clung to them as they marched away in spite of the disapproval of the colonel and the protests of their parents. Some of the fathers were able to drag their distracted daughters back but about thirty of the most persistent marched off with the men. The colonel, who did not wish to use force to get rid of this unwanted increment to his train of followers, resorted to the simple but effective method of allowing them no rations. For a few days the girls subsisted by sharing those of their boyfriends but with 'times of scarcity coming on afterwards, a coolness took place on both sides, as might be expected, and the damsels dropped off by degrees.'[5]

On the line of march there was not much time for dalliance. It was when the army was in billets, particularly if the period was prolonged, that the liaisons with the girls flourished. Mr Augustus Schaumann was a good-looking German commissary with blue eyes, fair hair and a rounded, rather jolly face, which displayed a deceptive air of innocence. He took pains with his appearance and his dress was neat. He was amusing and popular with his fellows and he liked women, with whom he had a considerable success.

When he was stationed in Olite he claimed to have had affairs with two daughters of a wealthy landowner, the wife of a Spanish colonel, a pretty girl of unspecified family and the spouse of an organist who enjoyed herself while her husband was playing in church.[6]

Many of those men who conducted illicit affairs would willingly have married the girls, but the better-class Portuguese and Spanish families, although they did not object to mild flirtations, were bitterly opposed to their daughters' marrying British husbands because of the religious differences. The only solution was elopement, which was attempted on more than one occasion. Wellington, however, frowned heavily on such escapades, which could not fail to create bad feeling between the army and the local population, a state of affairs which he wished to avoid at all costs. He let it be known that officers who misbehaved in this way would be placed under close arrest and, if necessary, handed over to the local authorities to be tried by their tribunals.

One of the reasons that fraternization was so easy for the British was that they enjoyed a far better reputation among the local people than the French had done. Major Sherer discovered this one morning when he was enjoying a solitary ride outside the small town of Alagrete in the province of Alemtejo. It happened to be the feast day of San Domingo and he came upon a party of villagers picnicking on the green after attending a mass in honour of the saint. He was welcomed and invited to join the party. Among the girls he particularly noted a blue-eyed beauty whose good looks were enhanced by a wide black hat lined with pink silk. Her dress was equally becoming. He entered into conversation with her mother who was delighted to hear that her daughter would be considered a very pretty girl even in England. She then expressed her joy that the country was now under the protection of the British army and that the French would be unable to return to destroy the country and insult the young women.[7]

Perhaps she was a little too credulous of British good behaviour. Some of the young men were far from trustworthy when confronted with the attractive girls. When the amorous Schaumann and a young doctor spent the night at the well-kept house of a hospitable widow in St Pedro they were at once fascinated by her sixteen-year-old daughter. The girl, Anna Joaquina, was a chambermaid to a countess in Lisbon and well able to deal with the advances of forward young men. She was home at the time to help her mother as it was the period of the vintage. She sang songs from the Lisbon opera for Schaumann and the doctor but, while encouraging their advances, skilfully held them at bay when they became too ardent. The mother, more observant and worldly wise than the lady of Sherer's acquaintance, was taking no chances and, when the household retired for the night, took care that her daughter's room was securely locked and bolted. It was as well that she did. Schaumann admits that he discovered these precautions with 'great distress' and that he had to be content with dreaming 'the whole night of Joaquina'.[8]

At the same time, there can be little doubt that the popularity of the British army with the ladies paid handsome dividends during the war. More than one young man was saved from the enemy by the bravery of a foreign girl. In 1810 Lieutenant MacCullogh was wounded and captured by the French when he was on duty in an advanced picquet. He refused to give his parole* as he had no intention of being locked up in a prisoner-of-war camp and hoped to make his escape before his captors could conduct him to the French frontier. Because of this refusal all his privileges as an officer were withdrawn and he was marched with the other-rank prisoners to Valladolid. During the march he managed to make friends with the French conducting officer. As a result, during the halt in Valladolid he was allowed to stay under guard in a private house instead of being confined in the town gaol. The daughter of the house was a young lady who was much impressed with the good looks of the handsome prisoner. She managed to communicate with him and promised to relate his plight to a university professor, who was known to carry out undercover work for the British. It was not long before MacCullough was delighted to be presented with the clothes of a Spanish peasant, a supply of dollars and, perhaps most pleasant of all, 'a kiss on each cheek burning hot from the lips of his preserver'. Thus equipped he was able to make his way back to the British lines where his adventure was the subject of much merri-

* The term 'parole' sprang from the French expression *parole d'honneur*, word of honour. A prisoner who gave his parole was considered to have promised that he would not attempt to escape or to fight again until he was officially exchanged with the enemy for one of their prisoners of equal rank. When parole had been given the prisoner was released from close arrest and allowed considerable freedom of movement.

ment. Wellington was so amused by the story of the escape that he insisted upon MacCullough, dressed in the peasant's costume, joining him for dinner.[9]*

It was not only their allies who helped the soldiers in trouble. When the army arrived in France, many French girls were equally willing to help. There was a small island in the River Adour and all its defensible positions were held by the French. One night a British party was sent over to reconnoitre these dispositions. A small patrol of five men worked its way up to a farmhouse, where one of the men had a girlfriend. He tapped on her window, which was cautiously opened by the girl and her mother. The two women were very nervous and explained that a large party of French soldiers was occupying the next house which was only a few yards distant. The girl, appalled at the danger her friend and his companions were in, then said that she would go to the house on some pretext and find out exactly how many of her countrymen were there. She was soon back with the alarming news that the French detachment consisted of an officer and sixty men. Notwithstanding the danger, the British patrol decided to shelter for the night in the farmhouse. They were made most welcome by their hostess whose only concern was that they should get away safely. This they achieved shortly before dawn the next morning.[10]

Not all the girls were asked to take risks like these, but romances can flourish just as easily without the spice of danger. Quite soon after the army's arrival in Portugal a number of local ladies had started to follow the drum. Some of them married soldiers and others joined the troops in less regular unions. Not all those who would have liked to marry a British soldier were successful. When the army was in Lisbon after the battle of Vimiero, Rifleman Harris was lodged in the house of a shoemaker. He was in charge of the regimental cobblers, who carried out their work in his landlord's shop. During his stay Harris lost his heart to the shoemaker's handsome daughter Maria, to whom he proposed marriage. The parents were completely in favour of the match but they wished to

---

* MacCullough's subsequent history was not so happy. He lost the use of one arm from a wound received during the pursuit of Massena in 1811. The other was blown off by one of the last rounds fired at the battle of Waterloo in 1815. He was then given brevet promotion to major over the heads of many officers who, though senior to him, unanimously approved of his preferment. Unfortunately he did not have long to enjoy his success. He died shortly afterwards in London as a result of his injuries.

impose two conditions before the wedding took place. These were that Harris should become a Catholic and desert from the colours so that he could remain with them as one of the family. These conditions were not at all acceptable to the prospective bridegroom who replied that he would have to remain with his regiment for the remainder of the war. When the fighting was over he would be able to get his discharge and then he would come back and marry Maria. It is to be hoped that the poor girl did not take these promises too seriously for Harris tells us that 'soon after this the army marched for Spain; the Rifles paraded in the very street where the shop I had so long worked at was situated, and I saw Maria at the window. As our bugles struck up, she waved her handkerchief; I returned the salute, and in half an hour had forgotten all about her. So much for a soldier's love.'[11]

Another lighthearted affair took place about the same time, when the flirtatious commissary Schaumann was on the road near Lisbon. He and some of his companions stopped to buy a turkey from a farmer's wife. As they were completing the transaction they noticed that the daughter of the house was a very pretty girl. They thereupon proposed that part of the deal should be that each of them should give and receive a kiss. The girl was delighted at receiving so much attention and had no objection to being embraced and bestowing her kisses. The ceremony, however, took rather longer than she expected since the last man to be kissed always hastened round to the end of the line to secure another caress. This pleasant game continued for some time and was much enjoyed by all concerned.[12]

This exchange of kisses for food was in no way unique. On one occasion Kincaid, whose mess had been without bread for three days, set off before daylight to see what he could buy in a village about two miles away. He was in luck. When he arrived, he discovered a party of nuns standing by the village oven waiting for some Indian corn loaves, which they had brought to be baked. He explained to them how short he and his companions were of bread, at which two of the nuns agreed to sell him their loaves. For these he gave them a dollar to share and a kiss apiece. He noted that they accepted his salutes as 'an unusual favour'.[13] In saying this he may have flattered himself. He was inclined to over-estimate his appeal to the sisters. On one occasion he boasted that he had never 'asked

A continental lady bringing a basket of cherries to sell to the soldiers.

Women searching for their loved ones on the battlefield.

The aftermath of battle.

A young French girl passing through British lines at Busaco in 1810, to help a captured general.

Agostina, the Spanish heroine of the siege of Saragossa.

Juana Maria de Los Dolores de Leon.

Harry Smith of the 95th (Rifle Brigade).

The Siege of Badejoz, 1812.

a nun or an attendant at a nunnery if she would not elope with me that she did not immediately consent and that too uncon-ditionally'.[14] This is a gasconade that does not really ring very true. A more attractive picture of the nuns and their life is given by Sherer who wrote that

> in another convent in that city [Portalegre] I remember a sister, neither young nor beautiful, but so interesting as to rivet attention and awaken all one's sympathy. She was not always herself, and, when in the fit of her strange melancholy, she would come to the gate and sing; sweetly indeed, but with a wildness that filled the eyes of those who heard her with tears. She never wept herself; but smiled often and most mournfully. She had been disappointed in love early in life, and sent into the convent; at least we heard so. I should like to have known her history; but on this she never spoke, and I respected her sorrow too much to pain her by an unguarded question. She was very fond of the English officers in whose countenances, at least in many, she might have observed an expression of manly pity, which soothed perhaps her wounded heart.[15]

Outside the walls of the convents, in the towns and villages, the friendly relations that grew up between the men and the girls contributed enormously to the success of the many dances that took place. These were organized by all ranks and varied from generals' balls to privates' improvised hops. They were arranged wherever the troops happened to be when hostilities were in abeyance. The Spanish girls were particularly popular. Kincaid, who, whatever his other qualities were, certainly had a roving eye, tells us that 'a Spanish peasant girl has an address about her which I have never met with in the same class of any other country; and she at once enters into society with the ease and confidence of one who has been accustomed to it all her life.'[16]

Some of the dances continued throughout the night. Tomkinson, of the 16th Light Dragoons, tells of a ball in April 1812 when the officers left the ballroom at daylight to mount their horses. They then took up their positions at the head of their troops and immediately marched out of the town.[17] By the time they reached France even the straitlaced Quartermaster Surtees was not altogether critical of the dancing habit. His complaint was that the morality of the French girls was not the highest in the world and that as 'they were generally more pleasing, they were the more seducing and consequently the more dangerous.' At the same time he found the French a gay and lively people and was sufficiently *au fait* with their 'several little balls and hops' to notice that 'the young men of his battalion were learning to dance quadrilles'.

Schaumann had no inhibitions about enjoying the dances. At Covilhão he was elected to be the grand steward of a ball given by the army to the local inhabitants. A suitable room in a battle-scarred palace was discovered and decorated with flowers. Vast quantities of appetizing food were procured and the regimental band of the 2nd Light Battalion of the King's German Legion engaged. When the preparations were well under way the organizers met with a major setback. The ladies of the town had suffered serious affronts at a previous dance given by the French when they were in occupation of the town. This had resulted in a deep distrust of all military men. The invitations to the dance were answered by refusals from all quarters. Tactful calls had to be made on the ladies' houses at which it was explained to them that the British would, of course, behave in a more decorous and respectful manner than their enemies. On hearing this the ladies withdrew their refusals and signified their intention of attending the ball.

When the night arrived the preparations were on a grand scale. The street leading to the palace was lined with soldiers carrying torches. Inside the building waiters, and troopers' wives all clad in their best dresses, stood ready to receive the guests. Mounds of cakes, fruit and other delicacies stood ready along the walls with a profusion of wine, claret cup and punch to wash the solids down. About seventy officers in their most colourful uniforms were present to greet the townspeople. Beside the scarlet and blue of the uniforms the Portuguese men looked somewhat drab, but the silk gowns of the ladies, bedecked with gold and jewels, enhanced the brilliance of the scene. A bizarre background was made up by large numbers of monks, children and beggars who had made their way in through the back premises to see the fun.

When the wine had flowed for some time all inhibitions were thrown aside and the dancing became progressively wilder. Many of the ladies pinned up their dresses so that they could move more freely. The men had no objection since those 'who had pinned up their dresses tightly in front of them, outlined their figures very sharply behind, while others, who had pinned them behind, produced the reverse effect.' Even such senior characters as the commander and the adjutant-general of the cavalry division were so carried away by the spirit of the occasion that they were to be seen taking part in the sarabands and fandangoes. It is to be hoped that the latter were not quite so indecorous as the fandangoes described by a Scottish soldier. He could

> hardly say it is a dance, for it is scarcely decent. The dancers run first to each other, as if they are looking for one another; then the woman runs away, the man follows; next he runs, and she follows. This they do alternately, all the time using the most expressive gestures, until both seem overcome, when they retire and another couple take their place. This dance had a great effect upon us; but the Spaniards saw it without being moved and laughed at the quick breathing and amorous looks of our men.[19]

While the dancers were hard at work on the floor, the less energetic guests were making heavy inroads into the refreshments. By eleven o'clock it became clear that the food was soon going to run out. Messengers were at once despatched into the town where all the available edibles were collected to replace the rapidly dwindling stocks. These kept the buffet going for another two or three hours at the end of which the majority of the revellers started to find their way home.[20]

The most celebrated and the grandest ball of the war was held at Ciudad Rodrigo in March 1813. Wellington used this entertainment for the dual purpose of demonstrating his pleasure at being created duke of the city, and at the same time making it the occasion of the investment of General Lowry Cole with the Order of the Bath. All the main civic dignitaries were invited as well as the senior officers of the British and Spanish armies. The planning and preparations were on the scale generally associated with the arrangements for a great battle. The food was prepared at Frenada, Wellington's headquarters. It was then transported to Ciudad Rodrigo in wagons and on mules, together with large quantities of claret, champagne and port. All the plate and silver that could be found in the area was borrowed and collected. The glass and crockery were brought from Almeida, a distance of twenty-five miles.

The ball was held in the largest house in the city, which, though it had some excellent rooms, had been badly damaged in the siege. The walls had a number of holes and, more dangerously, there was also a large hole in the floor of the ballroom. Military ingenuity soon dealt with these blemishes. It was discovered that some fine damask satin hangings, brought from the Palace of Ildephonso, were in a local store. These were borrowed and used to adorn the walls. The ballroom itself was decorated to look like a tent with yellow drapes bordered in silver, arranged in festoons to form an entrance. The supper rooms were silver and gold. The hole in the ballroom floor was covered with a carpet and a sentry was placed on guard to keep unwary dancers away from it.

Everyone considered the affair to be a great success despite the general opinion that the beauty of the ladies was, with a few exceptions, below average. The Spanish guests demonstrated some of their national dances and joined in the English country dancing that followed. There was a good measure of eating and drinking and by five in the morning many of the men were not very steady on their feet. The Prince of Orange was successfully chaired round the room but when an attempt was made to repeat the process with General Vandeleur, it proved too much and the general was dropped on the floor.

Wellington deserved the success his ball achieved. He had remained working in his headquarters at Frenada until three-thirty on the afternoon of the party. He then rode the seventeen miles to Ciudad Rodrigo in two hours, changed into his best uniform bedecked with all his orders, danced until three-thirty in the morning and rode back to Frenada by moonlight, arriving home at six a.m. Ever dutiful he was back at his desk by midday.[21]

Though the flirtations at the dances were mainly short and superficial, those in billets could become more serious and often had to be broken off by the parents. A budding romance of Surgeon Henry ran a typical course. At the time he was billeted in Aldea Galega, a village south of the Tagus on the road from Lisbon to

Elvas. He had originally been sent there as medical officer to a detachment of marines. When the majority of his charges departed, the inspector of hospitals apparently forgot to send him a new posting. This left him with little work and plenty of time on his hands. Under such circumstances his existence might have become somewhat dull and uninteresting had he not been housed in extremely comfortable quarters, the owner of which was the proud father of an exceptionally good-looking girl called Theodora. With so little to occupy his time it was not surprising that he soon embarked on a serious flirtation. The progress of this romance was much impeded by Theodora's aunt, a strict and alert old dragon, who lived in the house and was always on the watch. In the early stages of the affair, which were largely confined to the exchange of long and loving glances, the disapproval of the aunt was not too annoying. The trouble started when Henry, being smitten more and more deeply as the days passed, grew progressively bolder. Eventually he wrote a letter, which he gave to his trustworthy servant Antonio to deliver to Theodora. He was rather proud of this missive which he had composed in his best Portuguese and which contained many flowery phrases full of love and admiration. The main purpose of the note was to arrange a meeting at which Henry could pour out the tale of his love to his *inamorata* and persuade her of his undying devotion. The letter finished on a note worthy of Italian opera. In it Henry enclosed a fishing hook attached to a long thread. He besought Theodora to lower this from her window, which was immediately above his, with her answer attached. He instructed her to preserve the hook and line with the greatest care so that it could be used as the medium for further correspondence. The great effort Henry had put into this long letter might well have been completely wasted as unfortunately Theodora was unable to read. However, she managed to overcome this difficulty by employing a reliable friend to read the letter to her. After sending it off, Henry spent an anxious evening in his room as he waited for it to grow dark. Eventually his heart gave an extra beat as the hook descended carrying a beautiful red rose. This encouraging response led to a meeting on the stairs at which Henry employed the whole of his Portuguese vocabulary explaining the depth of his affection. Theodora was equally enthusiastic. Henry was allowed to kiss her hand and was considering an attempt on her lips when the romance was interrupted by the arrival of the strict old aunt. Theodora was terrified and tearfully begged her aunt not to tell her father. Henry resorted to flattery. He appealed to the aunt's generous and beautiful nature and implored her not to let the story go any further. Neither had any success. Henry was called a heretic and told to hold his tongue. Theodora received six hearty smacks on the backside and was hustled off to her room. This was a serious setback and looked like being the end of the affair. Henry was therefore surprised and delighted when the next night the fishhook again descended bearing another rose. His pleasure was short lived. The next day the chief magistrate asked him to call. When he arrived at the office he received a cordial welcome whose sweetness was somewhat impaired by a strong aroma of garlic and tobacco. The magistrate apologized profusely for bothering him but explained that, as a senior Portuguese general was expected in the town, it would be necessary to lodge him in the comfortable quarters that Henry had been enjoying. He added that of course everything would be done to find Henry satisfactory alternative accommodation. Henry realized that this was a completely bogus excuse for getting him out of the house and protested that it was quite unreasonable to turn him, the chief doctor and commandant, a permanent resident of the town, out of his quarters to provide accommodation for a visitor, however important, who only intended to stay one night. The magistrate was not to be persuaded and refused to alter his decision. Henry also stuck to his guns and said that he had no intention whatever of moving. Heated words were exchanged and the two parted company with the one vowing that he would use force to secure an eviction and the other affirming equally strongly that he would do likewise to remain where he was.

On returning to his quarters Henry mounted a marine guard at the door of the house with instructions to resist any attempt to move him. Matters remained in this state for the next two days during which there was no sign of the expected general's arrival. Henry was therefore in possession of the field and thought that he had won the battle. However, as has often been said, it is one thing to win a battle but quite another to win a war. The final victory lay with Theodora's parents. The poor girl was sent away to stay with relations and Henry never saw her again.[22]

Another Portuguese family, living in Lisbon succeeded in thwarting an ardent British suitor. In this case the young lady was of harder heart than Theodora and, unlike her, enjoyed her admirer's discomfiture. The young man, an infantry officer, had been convalescing in Lisbon, where he showed no great anxiety to be passed fit so that he could rejoin his regiment in the firing line. This may not have been due altogether to a lack of valour but because he had fallen violently in love with a rich, attractive and well-born young woman. Though she was delighted at his admiration her parents were not. They put every possible obstacle in the way of the lovers and forbade the young man to visit the house. Far from being discouraged by these difficulties, he countered them by setting up an observation post in the rear of the family mansion opposite the young lady's window. The couple were then able to carry on communication by means of a simple telegraphic system. This was eventually discovered by the parents who determined to teach the unwanted suitor a salutary lesson. In the words of the diarist, 'they determined to bring about by strategem that which neither threat nor remonstrance could effect.'

The young woman was removed from her room and for some evenings the young man on his nightly vigil saw nothing of his loved one. After a few unrewarding visits he was doubly excited when he reached his post and saw her, dressed in a well-known gown of pink lace, peering through the curtains of her window. As he hurried forward to see her better, the figure in the window retreated, leaving it open and unlatched. Regarding this as an invitation to enter, he found a ladder and climbed into the room. Inside all was dark but he was just able to discern a movement in a nearby armchair. He at once threw himself on to his knees in front of the chair and started to pour out the tale of his love. As he was doing so, the doors of the room were suddenly thrown open and a large body of ladies and gentlemen carrying lights crowded in. The unfortunate Romeo then discovered that he was kneeling before a large monkey dressed in a replica of his beloved's well-known dress. This was bad enough but was nothing to the mortification he felt when he saw that his young lady was among the spectators. She was thoroughly enjoying the trick that had been played on him and, rather than coming to his aid, started to chide him for deserting her for a monkey. He angrily rose to his feet and drew his sword, intending to despatch the unfortunate animal which had unwittingly caused him so much anguish. At this the guests again began to twit him, praising his great courage in attacking a helpless and unarmed creature. This was more than the young man could bear. He rushed from the room covered with shame and confusion. The story soon spread through Lisbon with the satisfactory result that the disappointed suitor, unable to endure the laughs at his expense, rejoined his regiment as soon as he could. It is to be hoped that, back on the battlefield, he soon forgot his false friend and recovered his self-esteem.[23]

A gunner subaltern, travelling across Spain to rejoin his battery, was equally unlucky in love. During his travels he had joined forces with Blakeney of the 28th Foot who was also making his way to the front. When they arrived at Reynosa they were billeted in a rich gentleman's house where they were delighted to discover that two lovely young ladies were also in residence. The gunner was soon head over heels in love with one of them, who responded eagerly to his advances. As she was the niece of a Spanish bishop there was no possibility of the young couple's obtaining approval for the marriage which they contemplated. They therefore decided on a dawn elopement. The girl disguised herself as a postilion. For this purpose the two subalterns lent her a new hat, a pair of doeskin breeches, some top boots and a smart whip. The night before the escape was to be made the officers invited the family to dinner and attempted to dull their senses by plying them with liberal helpings of mulled wine spiced with brandy. This would probably have sent them all soundly to sleep had the young lady's aunt not observed the exchange of amorous glances which put her on her guard.

As dawn broke the postilion crept downstairs. Her disguise suited her admirably despite the fact that the breeches had proved rather tight round the seat and thus had to be slit down the back and then held together by a system of cross lacing. All seemed set for a successful escape until, as the party made its way across the courtyard towards the stables, it was intercepted by the suspicious aunt and a posse of servants. The poor girl was apprehended and taken back to the house. The subalterns were banished. Even then their cup of misery was not quite full. At their next halt they were being entertained at a large dinner party. In the middle of the meal a parcel arrived. Their host insisted that they should open it immediately. When they did so, to their own horror but much to the amusement of the other guests, it was found to contain the postilion's clothing including the 'mutilated buckskins with the hussared rear face'. The whole story then had to be told and caused considerable laughter, especially when one young lady innocently enquired who had laced up the back of the breeches as the postilion obviously could not have done so herself.[24]

It was not always the parents who got the best of the argument. Kincaid of the Rifles proved more than a match for a mother in Elvas. He was allotted a billet in a pleasant part of the town. When he arrived to take up his quarters the mistress of the house refused to let him in. When it became apparent that, if she did not open the door, he would have no hesitation in knocking it down she tried another ruse. She told him that her daughter was dangerously ill in the only spare bed and that it was, therefore, impossible to accommodate him. He was too sharp to be put off by such an unlikely story which he countered by replying that he was a doctor and would examine the young woman immediately to see if he could help her. After some argument he was shown up to the bedroom where he found an extremely healthy young woman lying fully clothed on top of the bedclothes. Kincaid asked her how she was feeling, at the same time administering a sound slap in an appropriate place.

> Never did Prince Hohenlohe himself perform a miracle more cleverly; for she bounced almost as high as the ceiling, and flounced about the room, as well and actively as ever she did, with a countenance in which shame, anger, and a great portion of natural humour were so amusingly blended, that I was tempted to provoke her still further by a salute.

Mother and daughter could not help being amused by this instant treatment and accepted defeat in good part. Kincaid was allowed to remain without any further protests and, when he left, he relates, 'They told me I was the best officer they had ever seen, and begged that I would always make their house my home; but I was never fated to see them again.'[25]

When the army first moved into Spain it was delighted to discover that the beauty of the ladies was well able to bear comparison with that of the belles who had been left behind in Portugal. Schaumann was rapturous. He wrote that

> the Spanish women who went to mass were all dressed in black – the wealthy in silk, the others in camel hair, trimmed in velvet and lace. They wore white silk stockings and shoes, white gloves to the elbow, and short skirts with fringes six inches in length. Their calves were pretty, they had small kissable feet, and wore black veils which they held with two fingers in such a way as to conceal half their faces, and to leave only room for their dark eyes to flash between. Their hips were well developed, and their arms and breasts were full. But their waists made one long to clasp them, and their whole figures were charming, well rounded and slender. Their gait was regal.[26]

In Tarifa

> the ladies wore a narrow shawl or strip of silk, called a mantilla, generally black; the centre of this strip was placed on the crown of the head, the ends hanging down in front of the shoulders, the deep fringe, with which they were trimmed, reaching close to the ankle. So far this was common throughout Spain, but in Tarifa the ladies crossed the mantilla in front of their faces, by which the whole countenance was concealed, with the exception of one eye; this was done by dexterously lapping the mantilla across the waist, and so gracefully that the movement was scarcely perceptible. I have seen many English and even Spanish ladies of other provinces endeavour to imitate this sudden and graceful movement, but never without awkwardness; whereas every female in Tarifa accomplished it in a moment. This temporary disguise was resorted to when the ladies went out to walk, and so perfect was the concealment, and the dress of the ladies so much alike, that the most intimate acquaintances passed each other unknown. Thus accidents might happen and husbands fail to know their wives.[27]

Ladies like these were certain to attract and inspire affection. Surgeon Henry, who quickly recovered from his discomfiture over Theodora, was later posted to Truxillo, where he lived in the house of a Spanish count, a descendant of Pizarro and the father of two attractive daughters. Henry was soon infatuated with Donna Bernada, the younger and prettier of the girls. Though his days were fully occupied in the military hospital, which was full of sick and wounded soldiers, the evenings, which were devoted to 'dancing, forfeits, blind man's buff, lessons on Don Quixote, singing, the guitar and suchlike authorized modes of making love',[28] provided plenty of opportunity for flirtation. Furthermore,

> it is customary in Spain to take one's chocolate in bed very early in the morning, and as there is no harm in doing at Rome what the Romans do in such matters, I have found it good policy to conform to the national custom; Antonio would sometimes bring it to me, fuming and fragrant, by daylight. But more frequently the fairy-footed Bernada, accompanied by Francesca, would give a slight tap at the chamber door, and then appear at my bedside, bearing a little silver salver, on which was a small gilded cup of chocolate, so thick and rich that the little delicate parallelopiped of toast, its unvarying attendant, would stand upright in the middle. Then would the lovely sisters remain – 'twin cherries on one stalk' – in all honest confidence, laughing and joking, and lisping their beautiful language, till I had finished my chocolate – a matter which I was never in a hurry to accomplish.[29]

Henry is careful to add that it would have been impossible for two girls to have 'comported themselves with greater propriety'.

A stay of three months under such circumstances could not fail to bring a susceptible young man's passion to the boil. As his wooing intensified so did its difficulties. A jealous Spanish rival threatened his life. When the threats proved ineffective, the rival planned to have him killed when he was paying a night visit to a patient. A letter warned him of his danger and he was able to organize a small party of hospital orderlies. These lay in wait for the would-be assassins who were ambushed and given a good beating. The rival himself was further punished by the administration of a large dose of a strong purgative, which no doubt brought home to him the unwisdom of getting into the bad books of a medical man.

Suddenly, when the affair was at its height and Bernada had assured him that she was his for ever, Henry was ordered away to Elvas. As the count would certainly have forbidden them to marry, the lovers planned to elope and have the ceremony carried out by a priest in a village a few miles off. In preparation for the escape, as no suitable vehicle could be procured, Henry bought a quiet female donkey to carry Bernada to the priest. Everything seemed to be satisfactorily arranged for a successful departure when, at the very last moment, the donkey was kicked by an excited jackass and badly hurt. As it proved to be impossible to get another donkey at short notice and Henry could not delay his departure, Bernada was left weeping in her sister's arms. It is to be hoped that she soon recovered from her disappointment and found a nice young local husband. For Henry we need feel no sympathy. Though he was, of course, upset at first, he records that he soon realized how lucky he was that the kick of a donkey saved him from making an ass of himself.[30]

Sergeant Costello, on the other hand, was not at all pleased when he lost a girl friend as a result of the army's being ordered to retreat from Burgos in 1812. Before the withdrawal began he had become attached to a dark-eyed girl called Clementaria, sister of a guerrilla and full of hatred for the French. Costello had spent many an evening with her beneath the Spanish moon, singing serenades and learning to play the castanets. When the local population heard that the British were going to depart and leave their area to be reoccupied by the enemy that they loathed so much, they were exceedingly annoyed. Costello was refused a goodbye kiss, and the last words he heard from the pretty Clementaria were not of love but of scorn. 'Begone, you cowardly English,' she cried, 'you have not the courage to fight the enemy of our country; those who have butchered my dear father and brother.' She would have been even more enraged and upset could she have foreseen that in the course of time Costello would actually marry one of the hated enemy, a French girl called Augustine.[31]

Though Clementaria is to be praised for her patriotism, many Spanish girls were not so particular. Quite a few were more than willing to throw in their lot with the French soldiers. In the advance of 1813 Private Wheeler wrote home, 'We picked up many prisoners in a village, some in bed, others half-dressed. In a house I, with two of my comrades, found an officer and Spanish woman in bed. It was laughable to see him rub his eyes and stare at our red jackets.'[32] At the same time it would be unkind to reproach the girls for fraternizing with the enemy. Love takes little account of national boundaries. Instead of a collection of war trophies Sergeant Bourgogne kept, as a reminder of his long service, a little box 'containing rings, hair necklaces, and portraits of the mistresses he had had in all the countries he had visited'.[33]

In the case of Captain G[*], it would have been better for him if his lady love had said, 'Begone' instead of loving him too much. He had been wounded at the battle of Vitoria in June 1813, and, during his convalescence, met and took under his protection a young lady who lived in the city. Her brother was an officer in the Spanish army, and, outraged by the captain's treatment of his sister, he determined to punish him. Instead of challenging him to a duel, he gathered an escort of armed men and he set off to attack the captain in his quarters. The party arrived as Captain G was about to undress for bed. Hearing a noise in the passage, he left his room to see what was happening and was set upon by the Spaniards. Fortunately he had his sword and, singlehandedly, succeeded in putting the assassins to flight. As a result of their discomfiture they were more cautious when they returned later in the night. This time they remained outside the house and fired volleys through the door before the captain could get at them. He fell mortally wounded. His men were exceedingly indignant at this cowardly murder of a popular officer. They saw nothing very unusual or reprehensible in his treatment of the lady and thought that the Spanish authorities should be forced to make proper retribution.[34]

Naturally, when the war ended, many of the unions with the foreign girls had to be brought to an end. A few of the women who had followed the army were allowed to embark for England but the majority were returned to their homes (see Appendix F). A number of men were so attached to their 'wives' that they could not bear to leave them. Costello reported that:

> many men of our regiment bound by the charms of the signorettas who had followed their fortunes throughout the war, took this opportunity to desert their country's cause, to take up that of their Dulcineas. Among others were two of my company, who, not contented with the 'arms' offered by these 'invincibles',

[*] The identity of Captain G of the 94th (Scots Brigade) is tactfully concealed by Sergeant Donaldson in his *Recollections*.

took rifles and all with them, and we never saw or heard of them after.'[35]

Other men, who were not prepared to desert, were so affected by the separation that 'buckets full of salt tears were shed by men who had almost forgotten the way to weep.'[36]

Surtees has left us a vivid picture of the return to Spain and Portugal of the women who were left behind.

The departure of the poor women caused many heavy hearts, both among themselves, poor creatures, who had a long and dreary journey before them, and among those with whom they had lived and who had shared in all their good and bad fortune; but among these, several on both sides were not oppressed with too fine feelings. A friend of mine, who was an officer in the Portuguese service, told me afterwards that the women marched down to Spain and Portugal at the same time as his regiment did; that they formed a column of 800 or 900 strong; that they were regularly told off into companies; and that the commanding officer, a major, and all the captains, were married men who had their families with them – all excellent arrangements; but that they were the most unmanageable set of animals that ever marched across a country. The officers had to draw rations for them all the way; but many of them, he said, left the column and went wherever they pleased. Few reached Portugal in the order they started.

Chapter

EIGHT

JUANA MARIA DE LOS DOLORES DE LEON

IN the early nineteenth century the aftermath of a siege was often a horrifying affair. The assaulting troops, after enduring great danger and acute discomforts during the preparation period, invariably suffered heavy casualties when the assault was finally launched. When they got into the town their blood was up and they considered the just reward for their persistence and bravery was the right to pillage the captured city.

At the siege of Badajoz in 1812, the soldiers had had to work with poor quality tools in flooded trenches under a constant downpour. Because of inadequate transport there had been problems in keeping them supplied with food and ammunition. These wretched conditions had lasted from 17 March, when the investment began, until 6 April when the assault was launched. This began at ten o'clock on a moonlight night and the illumination was increased by immense fireballs which the French hurled from the walls to give themselves a better view of the storming parties. On top of the breaches they had fixed obstacles made of razor-sharp swords, and as the assaulting regiments tried to get forward they were met with a barrage of shells and exploding powder barrels. The resulting carnage was appalling. In forty attempts not one allied soldier managed to cross the barrier of swords. At length, with great difficulty, the 3rd and 5th Divisions managed to establish ladders on the ramparts and break into the town.

The capture of Badajoz covered the army with glory but this glory was soon to be tarnished. 'The atrocities committed by our soldiers on the poor innocent and defenceless inhabitants of the city no words suffice to depict.'[1] There were reasons, if no excuse, for this. The men had had a particularly bad time and as usual after an assault were half wild with a desire for vengeance, but there was more to it than that. They sensed that the Spanish civil population of the town had done more for their enemies than their friends and they were burning with indignation. As Sir William Napier, the great contemporary historian of the war, says, 'The possession of Badajoz had become a point of personal honour with the troops of each nation, but the desire for glory with the British was dashed by a hatred of the citizens on an old grudge; recent toil and hardship with much spilling of blood had made many incredibly savage.'[2] Moreover, there is some reason to believe that the troops genuinely understood that they were to be allowed to sack the town. Sergeant Donaldson, for example, records in his account that 'when the town surrendered, and the prisoners were secured, the gate leading into the town from the castle was opened and we were allowed to enter the town for the purpose of plundering it.'[3]

Whatever the reason, the capture of the town was followed by a complete breakdown in discipline which practically amounted to a mutiny. For three days the troops raged through the streets completely out of control, drinking, raping and looting. The officers were unable to exercise any influence on them. The houses were filled from cellar to garret with drunken soldiery in quest of more liquor, and intent on robbing the inhabitants of every penny they could find. The din and confusion were indescribable, being composed of a medley of drunken shouts, the appalling shrieks of terrified women, the smashing of woodwork as doors were beaten down, and the discharge of firearms which were being recklessly fired in all directions.

Out of this inferno two ladies managed to escape. As they tried to flee from the city they were lucky enough to encounter John Kincaid and Harry Smith, two young officers of the 95th (Rifle Brigade). The elder lady explained that she was the wife of a Spanish officer who was away at the war. She was possessed of ample means and lived in the town in a large and comfortable manor house. This had been wrecked by the looters, who had also stolen their jewellery. Their ears were still bleeding from the rough treatment they had received when their earrings were torn off. The elder woman was terrified that her young fourteen-year-old sister would fall into the hands of the licentious soldiery. She appealed to the two officers for help and protection. Smith and Kincaid were both immediately overcome by the charm of the young girl who, though not beautiful, had flashing eyes and a superb figure, which her Spanish costume set off to perfection.[4]

The amusing and easy-going Kincaid confessed that he had fallen in love with her as soon as he had seen her, but that he had kept his mouth shut when it became apparent that she preferred his friend Smith. In this she was either very lucky or very clever, for Smith, though ten years her senior and a vain and somewhat self-satisfied character, proved to be the most constant and adoring of husbands. He also enjoyed in the days to come a far more colourful and successful career than his potential rival.

The courtship was short and sweet; in two days they were married and Juana was as good a wife as Harry was a husband. No spouse could have been more single-minded or self-effacing in encouraging him in his career. The difference in religions, which might have been divisive, was removed when some years later Juana conformed to the Church of England. Many of Smith's friends thought that this early marriage might prove to be the end of his promising career. In this they were very wrong.

After the capture of Badajoz the army was soon once more on the move. Harry then discovered that his child bride knew little or nothing about riding anything more spirited than one of the local donkeys. Never one to be put off by minor difficulties, he solved this problem by employing a horse artillery saddler to convert one of his saddles into a side saddle. He then mounted Juana on a quiet but otherwise indifferent Portuguese charger, with the promise that she would be promoted to his favorite Andalusian horse as soon as she could ride as well as she sang and danced. This was a tall order but she proved so apt a pupil that in a few weeks she was riding 'Tiny', who carried her to the end of the war.

Juana accompanied Harry through the long and tedious marches that preceded the battle of Salamanca in 1812. The night before the battle she slept on a bed of damp green wheat holding the horse's reins in her hands. Being young, she was still able to laugh when she woke to find that the ungrateful beast had eaten the greater part of her bedding while she was asleep. During the fighting Harry sent her to the rear with his trustworthy groom, West, and a spare horse in case of accidents.

After the great victory Harry was given a fortnight's leave in order to recover from a painful attack of boils. A short stay in the beautiful city of Salamanca made a pleasant change for a young couple who had up to then passed the whole of their married life enduring the rigours of an army in the field. They managed to enjoy themselves although they had to forgo any sort of extravagance and lived mainly on their rations. Owing to a shortage of funds the army's pay was well in arrears and the Smiths had very little in their purse. Unfortunately, this enjoyable rest did nothing to cure Harry's boils and, worse still, it had to be followed by four days' hard riding to enable them to catch up with his brigade. They managed to reach Madrid in time to witness Wellington's entry and were impressed by the enthusiasm of the townspeople at this spectacular event. During their stay in the capital Harry delighted in showing off his wife on the Prada, where, in his eyes at any rate, she outshone all the local beauties.

After the failure to capture Burgos, the Smiths were involved in the retreat to Ciudad Rodrigo, which started in torrential rain. They were accompanied by the vicar of Vicalbaro, who had sought their protection as he was unpopular with the French and feared to stay behind after the departure of the British. Their first night was a foretaste of the discomfort they would have to endure throughout the withdrawal. It was spent in a minute hovel about six foot square which the Smiths shared with the Spanish padre and Harry's thirteen greyhounds. Nevertheless, the padre proved to be a most useful addition to the party as his presence enabled them to purchase from time to time such luxuries as extra bread, chocolate, sausages and eggs to supplement the ration. In a region of scarcity, money alone, without clerical influence, would not have been sufficient to obtain these welcome commodities.

During the long and wearing retreat Juana had every reason to be thankful that she had been allowed to take over her clever new horse. On one particular day they had to cross the high-banked River Huebre. Tiny jumped fearlessly in and carried Juana to the other side. When the unfortunate vicar attempted to follow, his pony lost his feet and was drowned. The padre himself was saved only because, as he floated down the stream, his capacious cloak kept him afloat until some soldiers were able to rescue him. 'His holiness', Smith remarked, 'began now to think I had not exaggerated the hardships of a soldier's life.'[5] Damp and miserable, the priest asked Smith's groom to lend him Harry's spare charger but, in spite of Juana's support for her distressed countryman, West was too old a soldier to comply with such a request. 'Never lend master's other fighting horse, not to nobody,' he said, adding rather unkindly, 'night and the walk will warm you.'

Even when they were safe on the far side of the river their troubles were far from over. They were soon involved in a heavy skirmish with the enemy's advanced guard in which a captain of the 52nd was killed and between forty and fifty men wounded. They were in a sorry state when Harry, who as brigade major had been sent back to hurry on the 52nd Regiment of Foot, discovered them. Juana was wet through after her river crossing and the padre more than half drowned. They were all greatly relieved and much happier when they managed to install themselves in a billet which, though it would have seemed a pretty miserable abode at other times, now enabled them to light a fire, dry their clothes and prepare some food.

After this the pressure on the rearguard grew less severe and life became correspondingly easier. It was discovered that the padre was a more than capable cook and he and Juana had a lot of amusement comparing their skills. At last the retreat came to an end. The Smiths then found themselves quartered in the village of Fuentes d'Oñoro at the home of Maria Josepha, a tragic girl of whom we shall hear more in a later chapter.

After a winter devoted by Harry largely to hunting and coursing, the Smiths were again on the move. On 21 May 1813 they set off at daylight and marched for nineteen successive days. The start of the journey was far from auspicious. Of their five horses, three, including Tiny, were lame. If his general had not come to his aid with the occasional loan of a charger, Harry would have been hard put to it to keep himself mounted. To carry Juana he had to expend £140 on a good-looking thoroughbred. Unfortunately it proved to have more beauty than brain and fell clumsily on a bank near Palencia, breaking a small bone in Juana's foot in the process. This became very painful and there was a worrying moment when it looked as if she would have to be left behind until the foot recovered. As she was determined that they should not be separated she asked Harry to obtain a mule and a Spanish saddle, which would allow her to ride with her foot resting on a wooden board. This was done. It was an admirable solution for Juana but did little to improve the quality of the staff work at brigade headquarters. At the end of each day's march many of the staff officers were to be seen vying with one another for the opportunity to help her dismount instead of attending to their duties.

> Oh, the ceremony of her dismounting, the quantity of officers' cloaks spread for her reception; the 'Take care! Now I'll carry the leg,' of the kind-hearted doctor! Talk of Indian attention! Here was a set of fellows ready to lay down their lives even to alleviate momentary pain.[6]

At the battle of Vitoria on 21 June 1813, Harry's brigade was in support of the 7th Division and acquitted itself well. Towards the end of the fighting his horse was knocked off its feet by the wind pressure of a passing cannon shot. News filtered back to Juana that Harry had fallen and was dead. Miserable and in the deepest despair, she hurried forward with her groom to try and find the body. Not knowing that the brigade had been detached to the 7th Division she went in the wrong direction and it was not until she came up with the 1st Light Brigade that she was put on to the right road. It was nightfall before she found her husband and was overjoyed to discover that both he and his charger were none the worse for their unpleasant experience.

The night following the battle was spent in a barn which was also occupied by the brigade commander and his staff. Everyone was so tired that they all fell asleep without attempting to have a meal. At daybreak they were all on the move again. Just as they were about to mount their horses Juana heard the groaning of a wounded man. On investigation it was discovered that twenty French officers, who had been left behind when their army retired, were sheltering in the loft above the barn. One had died during the night, the remainder were wounded, many severely. They were unattended except for one Spanish woman who was doing her best to make them comfortable. Juana immediately went to her assistance; some breakfast was provided and everything possible was done to reduce the suffering of the wounded men. The Spanish lady, who was the mistress of one of the Frenchmen, was so overcome with gratitude to Juana for her kindness and help, that she insisted on presenting her with 'a most beautiful little pug dog, a thoroughbred one, with a very extraordinary collar of bells about its neck'.[7] This little animal, which was at once named 'Vitoria', later became the close companion of the horse Tiny and the universal pet of the soldiers in the division.

During the advance over the Pyrenees, General Vandeleur, the brigade commander and a great friend of Harry and Juana, was transferred to a cavalry brigade. He was replaced by General Skerrett, whom they found less congenial. His ADC, 'Ugly Tom Fane', on the other hand, was a very good-natured creature, who messed with the Smiths and accepted in good part the numerous little tricks that Juana delighted in playing on him. When a few months later the new brigade commander came into a substantial inheritance and returned to England they were all delighted. Harry and Juana were particularly pleased that his successor, Colonel Colborne, retained Ugly Tom as his ADC.

The marching through the Pyrenees was arduous and exhausting. Harry, writing of one such march, says:

> On the Pyrenees as on other mountains the darkness is indescribable. We were on a narrow mountain pass, frequently with room for only one or two men, when a soldier of the Rifle Brigade rolled down a hill as nearly perpendicular as may be.[8]

At the end of one particularly tiring day the Smiths and Ugly Tom lodged in the comfortable cottage of a good-natured farmer whose wife provided them with a sumptuous dinner of duck and green peas.

> We had a supper royalty would have envied . . . My wife had spread her cloak on the floor – she was perfectly exhausted – and was fast asleep. I awoke her, she ate a capital supper, but the next morning upbraided me and Tom Fane for not having given her anything to eat; to this day she is unconscious of sitting at our supper table. Judge by this anecdote what real fatigue is.[9]

At this period in the war a curious organization had evolved in the Light Division. Nearly every officer had acquired a number of goats and a small boy to look after them. When the division was on the move the goats were herded into brigade flocks. The boys on their own initiative used this as an excuse to organize themselves on military lines. They appointed a 'captain' to take charge and detailed regular guards. The sentries were armed with long white sticks and their period of duty was strictly controlled. Juana, who was fascinated by these urchins, took a great interest in them and their arrangements. From time to time she had long conversations with the captain, who used to consult her on questions of military procedure. At the end of the war, when the boys returned to Spain and Portugal, they were all given the goats that had been in their charge. The Smith's herdsman, who was called Antonio, in this way became the proud owner of a flock of fifteen and could look forward to becoming a substantial goat-proprietor.

As the advance through the Pyrenees continued, Harry's brigade took part in an attack on the heights of Vera. This was on 7 October 1813 and, in addition to its three British battalions, the brigade had a Portuguese regiment, the 1st Cacadores, commanded by Colonel Algeo. This officer's charger was very similar in appearance to one belonging to Harry. The resemblance of the two horses was the cause of Juana being subjected to a most alarming experience. She was watching the progress of the attack from a cottage window just outside musketry range when she saw

> this horse gallop to the rear, dragging for some distance the body by the stirrup. The impulse of the moment caused her with one shriek to rush towards it and so did her anxiety and fright add to her speed that my servant for some time could not overtake her. The horse came on, when she soon recognized that it was poor Algeo's charger, not mine, and fell senseless from emotion, but soon recovered, to express her gratitude to Almighty God.[10]

Though she had quickly recovered from her faint, it had been a fearful shock and she did not fully regain her usual composure for several days.

She had another scare shortly before Christmas 1813, during the advance towards Bayonne. It was on a day in which Colborne, not at all typically, had been somewhat slow in forming up his brigade to meet an enemy attack. As a result he was surprised and beaten back. The French came on so fast that Juana, who was in the rear of the fighting line, only had time to slip on her riding habit and mount her horse to escape capture. In the confusion most of the Smiths' baggage, a goose they were fattening for Christmas, and Vitoria, the pug dog, were lost. Fortunately for Vitoria she was recognized by a quick-witted bugler of the 52nd and rescued. The goose and the baggage were never seen again. Despite this setback the Christmas meal was a great success. Juana managed to produce an excellent meal, which was further improved by Harry's tactical skill. He invited as a guest the brigade commissary, who brought with him a plentiful supply of champagne to add to the feast.

After the army had crossed the River Adour and moved forward, Juana rode over the battlefield. She was horrified at the number of dead and dying who were left lying on the ground. Feeling miserable from this dismal experience she had still to endure a long and tiring ride. As darkness approached it became bitterly cold, sleet was falling and there seemed little prospect of finding any shelter. Eventually Harry discovered a small cottage near Mont de Marsan, which belonged to a poor French widow. They were in real luck. The widow made them more than welcome, lit a fire for them and produced a bowl of hot soup, which she served from a beautiful Sèvres basin of which she was very proud. It had been given to her as a wedding present and had not been used since her husband died. She turned out to be a fervent royalist and was anxious to show the British how grateful she was to them for rescuing her country from the tyrant Bonaparte. The next day the brigade was ordered to fall back on St Sèvere. The Smiths, who had a long march in bad weather in front of them, exchanged an affectionate farewell with their kind hostess in which expressions of mutual goodwill were reciprocated. That night they spent in a small deserted cottage by the roadside. The next morning, expecting a rapid move, they sat down to an early breakfast. Harry relates that while Juana was telling General Barnard, who had shared the cottage with them, of

> the kindness she had received the previous night and the history of the basin, to our horror in came my servant, Joe Kitchen, with the identical slop-basin full of milk. The tears rolled down my wife's cheeks. Barnard got into a storming passion. I said, 'How dare you, sir, do anything of the sort?' (He was an excellent servant.) 'Lord, sir,' he says, 'why the French soldiers would have carried off the widow, if she had been young, and I thought it would be so nice for the goat's milk in the morning; she was very angry, though 'cos I took it.'[11]

When a little later word arrived that no further move would be made until the next day, Juana immediately sent for her horse and her groom. When they came round she told Harry that she was going to visit a wounded officer. Her actual destination was the cottage at Mont de Marsan and her object to return the widow's basin. To do this she had to make a round trip of thirty miles along filthy roads in bad weather with an appreciable risk of being captured by a French patrol. The widow was overjoyed to recover her bowl and Juana was delighted that a wrong had been put right. When the story spread through the division, Juana was hailed as a true heroine. Few of the men would have wished to embark on such an arduous and risky ride, which had been voluntarily undertaken by a teenage girl.

In spite of her kindness, bravery and popularity, which it might have been supposed would have rendered her immune from personal attack, shortly after the episode of the bowl, Juana had a nasty fright. She was in billets in Gee. One morning she was waiting for the word that it was time to mount and join the column. As she sat alone in her room the old housekeeper of the billet stole in, seized her in a tight grip and said that she was going to kill her. It is quite probable that she would have succeeded in doing so had Harry's servant not arrived on the scene at the critical moment with the news that the move had been postponed. It was then discovered that, if anything upset the housekeeper, she became mad with rage. On this occasion she had been upset in the servants' quarters and had determined to get her revenge by attacking Juana. The delay in the projected move meant that the Smiths had to remain in the billets a further three days. During this period no further risks were taken. Juana's maid, Jenny Bates, a muscular wife of a soldier in the 52nd, was ordered never to leave her mistress's side.

When peace was signed in April 1814 the Smiths were quartered in Toulouse. They soon noticed a complete reversal in the numerical balance of the sexes. During the war there had been a scarcity of attractive young women, now there was an abundance. The majority of young Frenchmen had been conscripted for the army, leaving Toulouse full of pretty ladies, who were only too eager to welcome and fraternize with the victorious newcomers. A jealous Frenchman told an English officer, 'You have nothing to do now but to make the most of your advantages and enjoy yourselves; all the beauties have now declared for you.' There was no hesitation in following his advice. Young men, who for years had been deprived of the enjoyment of female society under peacetime conditions, were delighted to meet the advances of the local ladies. Many soon imagined they were in love and Harry Smith rejoiced that, in having his own delightful wife, he was free from such distraction. The city was soon a whirl of gaiety with a succession of theatres, fêtes and balls. Juana, who was a beautiful dancer, was much in demand at the latter.

This festivity was not to last long for the Smiths. Harry was almost immediately posted to America, where the British had been at war since 1812. He had not yet been promoted to substantive major and thought he would have a better chance of achieving this if he saw some more active service. Juana, who was not allowed to accompany him across the Atlantic, was sent back to England. She was escorted on the journey by Harry's brother, Tom, who suffered from a stiff leg, the result of a wound sustained at the battle on the Coa four years previously. The separation, though painful, was short. Harry was only in America for a few months. After taking part in the battle of Bladensburg and the capture of Washington in 1814, he was sent back to England as the bearer of the despatch announcing the British success. While he was away Juana lived in London, where she was able to see as much as possible of their mutual friends and get the latest news about Harry and the progress of the war.

The young couple were overjoyed to be reunited and even more pleased when it was known that the reward for their separation was the coveted step to Harry's majority. His mother had died during his absence. His first act was now to introduce Juana to his father. The meeting was an unmitigated success. Father and daughter-in-law took an immediate liking to each other. They became and from then on remained the firmest of friends. On this visit Juana was also reunited with Tiny who, when he came home from France, had been sent direct to Harry's father. To the family's amusement the horse recognized Vitoria the pug dog and the two animals were delighted to see each other again.

After three weeks' blissful leave Harry was again off to the wars. He was to return to America as assistant adjutant-general to Sir Edward Packenham. After taking part in the unsuccessful attack on

New Orleans he was once more sent back to England, arriving in time to be sent overseas again to take part in the Waterloo campaign. His second return from America was unannounced. An unwitting neighbour, who had seen him arrive but had not recognized him, told Juana as she was coming out of church that a chaise with a military looking passenger had just galloped up to her father-in-law's house. Juana, fearing that this might be a messenger bringing news that Harry had been killed or wounded, swooned on the spot. Her sisters-in-law managed to bring her round and were then able to tell her that it was Harry himself who was in the chaise. This brought her fully to her senses; she sprang to her feet, ran the whole way home and hurled herself into her husband's outstretched arms. They were not to be separated again for another twenty years.

Harry was overjoyed when he heard of the escape of Napoleon from Elba. It brought promotion to lieutenant-colonel within measurable distance. He at once set out for Belgium accompanied by his wife, brother, two grooms, five horses and a lady's maid, whom he lists in that order. The party landed at Ostend and travelled to Ghent where they remained until the French army crossed the frontier. Harry's brigade then marched through Brussels to Epernay, at the entrance to the forest of Soignies. When, on the morning of the battle of Waterloo, the brigade moved forward to join General Picton's division, Juana made her way back to Brussels. There she found the faithful West guarding her baggage and together they rode about five miles along the road to Antwerp. It was now about five in the morning and Juana decided to halt and have some breakfast. The baggage was unloaded and West went into an inn to buy some food. Suddenly the alarm was raised that the enemy was approaching. Juana ran to remount her horse, which had become very restive from the excitement and confusion that was going on all round. When she was back in the saddle she dropped the reins to take the pug dog from West. He, not realizing that she had done so, let go of the horse which immediately bolted. After an eight-mile gallop the stampeding animal almost ran into a wagon that was lying upset in its path. However, it was too big an obstacle to jump and at the last moment the horse pulled up with a jerk, throwing Juana and her dog over its head. Fortunately she managed to hold on to the reins and to climb back into the saddle complete with dog. This time she kept a firm hold of the horse's head and the only damage sustained was to her habit, which was covered with mud. After this disturbing incident she reached Antwerp wet through but otherwise unhurt. She was put up in the port by the wife of the garrison commander, who was able to lend her a dry, if rather voluminous, change of clothing.

The next day Juana's maid, baggage and spare horses arrived. She was delighted to see them though her mind was still full of anxiety about Harry. As she was too worried to be able to sleep, she got up at three in the morning on the 20th and set off with West for Brussels. Here the aftermath of the battle of Vitoria was repeated. She met some soldiers of the 95th who told her that Brigade-Major Smith had been killed. As the men were in Harry's regiment, she was in utter despair until she met a friend who was able to reassure her that it was another Smith that had been killed. Harry was safe and at Bavay. Thrilled at hearing this, she rode on to Mons where she arrived at midnight after a ride of sixty miles. Even so she allowed herself only the shortest of rests before continuing her journey to Bavay where she was reunited with Harry as dawn broke.

By this time the fighting was virtually over. The army moved on to Paris. The Smiths were lucky to secure a comfortable house at Neuilly and settled down to an enjoyable social life: 'Nothing but parties at night and races by day.' For his part in the campaign Harry was promoted to lieutenant-colonel and made a Companion of the Bath. Their existence seemed quite perfect until, at the beginning of 1816, Juana became seriously ill. For three days Harry feared that she was going to die, but her youth and sound constitution pulled her through. They remained in France for a further two years with Harry as Town Major of Cambray. They then returned to England.

In later life Harry Smith commanded the forces at the battle of Aliwal; he became Governor of the Cape of Good Hope; rose to the rank of lieutenant-general and was created Knight Grand Cross of the Bath.

NINE

WOMEN IN ADVERSITY

THE romances and elopements, the dances and flirtations were welcome diversions in the usually sombre and often harsh lives of the men and women involved in Wellington's campaigns. There was a moment when Private Wheeler, by no means a gloomy man, wrote in a letter to his family, 'My thoughts are so much occupied with the misery and misfortune of so many of my comrades and their wives I cannot get into any other strain.'[1] This mood is also expressed by Sergeant Donaldson who wrote that

> during our campaigns in the Peninsula, it is almost incredible what the poor women who followed us had to endure, marching often in a state of pregnancy, and frequently bearing their children in the open air, in some instances on the line of march, by the road side; suffering, at the same time, all the privations to which the army was liable. In quarters, on the other hand, they were assailed by every temptation which could be thrown in their way, and every scheme laid by those who had rank and money, to rob them of that virtue which was all they had left to congratulate themselves upon.[2]

Mrs McGuire knew how hard life could be. When she started on the long retreat to Corunna she was already in an advanced stage of pregnancy. From the beginning of the march the conditions were dreadful. At one time the road lay under deep snow, at another it was covered with heavy mud and slush. Shoes were soon worn out or were sucked off the wearer's feet. Marching became a painful process. The cold never let up and there was practically no shelter. Despite these difficulties Mrs McGuire struggled on. At length one evening, utterly wretched and worn out, she was unable to take another step. She left the disordered column and lay down upon the ground a little way off the road. Her husband, seeing her distress, followed her out of the ranks and went over to where she lay. The soldiers, who had grown hardened to such pitiful sights, remarked to each other that that was the last that would be seen of the unhappy couple. Night was coming on and death was the usual lot of those who, unable to keep up with the column, were left out in the open. Moreover, the enemy were not far behind and those stragglers who managed to survive were likely to be taken prisoner.

Some short time later the men of the rear party were surprised to see McGuire and his wife hurrying after them. A few minutes later, when the McGuires caught up with them, surprise turned to astonishment as it was seen that the wife was carrying a newly-born baby in her arms. The infant had practically no covering and in the biting cold it was not to be expected that, in spite of its mother's courage and resolution, it would survive the night. Nature mercifully decreed otherwise. Husband and wife, taking turns to carry the child, succeeded in preserving him right through the terrible retreat. They brought him safely down to the coast and on to a transport. Their bravery was properly rewarded. The babe survived a tempestuous voyage home and grew up to be a strong and healthy young man.[3]

There was yet another example, in 1812, of a baby's surviving one of the many roadside births. A baggage party moving north from Lisbon was accompanied by a number of wives hoping to rejoin their husbands, who had taken part in the advance to Burgos and the subsequent retreat. One, who was in the last stages of pregnancy, had been abandoned by the roadside 'in a ravaged and deserted countryside where wolves abounded' to produce her child. Luckily for her, she was found by a passing British officer who paid an old Portuguese peasant woman to assist her. When the baby was born the peasant brought her food and found her shelter. The next day the mother walked seven miles to Pombal, the nearest town, carrying her infant in her arms. She was looked after in Pombal until she was able to move forward with another convoy to meet her husband. The peasant, who had been so much more helpful than the other British wives with the convoy, was suitably rewarded by the officer who had found the abandoned woman.[4]

A more tragic note was struck by Rifleman Harris after another episode he observed on the retreat to Corunna. He said that it was a sight that would remain with him to his dying day. His regiment had just moved off after a halt in a turnip field when his attention was caught by the screams of a little boy. The miserable child was being dragged along by his mother but he was so exhausted that his legs would no longer carry him. The mother, who was herself almost at the end of her tether, no longer had the strength to pick him up in her arms. Some men who had helped her earlier in the day had barely sufficient stamina left to keep themselves moving. The end was inevitable. The little boy stumbled and fell to the ground with his worn-out mother. As the column marched on, the two exhausted bodies were left lying where they were, adding to the trail of dead and dying which marked the passage of the army. The concluding words of Harris's account of this distressing episode make painful reading:

> This was not the only scene of the sort I witnessed among the women and children during the retreat. Poor creatures! They must bitterly have regretted not having accepted the offer to embark at Lisbon for England, instead of accompanying their husbands into Spain. The women, however, I have often observed, are most persevering in such cases, and are not to be persuaded that their presence is often a source of anxiety to the corps they belong to.[5]

All those who took part in this retreat have left accounts of how terrible the conditions were. Schaumann, in *On the Road with Wellington*, explained that 'every minute a horse would collapse beneath its rider and be shot dead. The road was strewn with dead horses, bloodstained snow, broken carts, scrapped ammunition boxes, cases, spiked guns, dead mules, donkeys and dogs, starved and frozen soldiers, women and children.'

The French women suffered similarly during their retreat from Moscow in 1812. For example, there was Madame Dubois, the wife of a regimental barber, whose child was born one evening in the shelter of a wood. Heavy snow was falling at the time and the cold was intense, with twenty degrees of frost. Luckily there was a doctor nearby who was able to attend her, and the regimental commander, Colonel Bodel, lent her his coat to provide some sort of shelter for the night. In the morning she was able to acquire the cloaks of two men who had died of cold and was glad to wear them both. The baby was wrapped in a sheepskin. When the march recommenced the colonel lent her his horse. Few would have envied her her plight, though compared with many others she was a lucky woman.[6]

A pitiful incident of a different kind took place during the 1812 retreat from Burgos. There was one young wife who had followed her husband throughout the campaign. She had been present at the battle of Salamanca and had trudged the whole way across Spain to Burgos. When the long retreat started she continued to follow her husband's regiment, keeping as close to him as she could. The day came when she was so overcome by fatigue and hunger that she felt unable to walk any further. She told her husband that her strength was exhausted and that there was nothing left for her to do but collapse on the ground and await her end. Her husband told her that, if she was to survive and return with the army to its base, it was essential that she kept up with the column. He persuaded her to make one more effort, at the same time putting his arm round her to support her and help her on her way. For a short time he managed to keep her on her feet, but she was too weak to go far even with his help and soon found herself quite unable to drag one leg after the other. Her husband was given leave to fall out from the ranks so that he could remain with her and try to find her a place in one of the wagons that were following in the rear. When the wagons arrived they were already overloaded and there was no room for her. The drivers said that they had already passed many others who were unable to keep going. They had had to leave them lying exhausted by the wayside where they would either die or be captured by the French. The husband was now in despair, not knowing what to do. If he remained he would be taken prisoner and then be unable to help his wife; if he left her she would inevitably fall into the hands of the enemy. As he stood there trying to make up his mind, the unhappy girl pleaded with him not to leave her. He wished with all his heart to stay by her side but he could not bear to think that, if he did so, his comrades might look on him as a deserter. After some hesitation he decided he must go. With a broken heart he bade farewell to his wife telling her that he must leave her and rejoin the colours. He never saw her or heard of her again. He never fully recovered from the trauma of making this terrible decision, he constantly brooded on it and the memory of his wife lying alone and exhausted by the side of the road embittered him for the rest of his life.[7]

Great as the responsibility of having a wife at the war must have been, Rifleman Howans was no doubt more than glad to have his wife to tend him after he had suffered from the brutality of General Craufurd. During Sir John Moore's retreat, when men and women were perishing on all sides from hunger and exhaustion, Craufurd heard Howans complaining that it would be more to the point if the general got them something to eat instead of constantly harassing them. Craufurd turned on him in a rage and ordered an instant court-martial, at which Howans was sentenced to three hundred lashes. The brigade marched all through the night and, when it halted the following morning, the men were formed into a hollow square to watch Howans receive his flogging. Howans, who was a very tough customer, took his punishment without a sound but, when it was over, his back was so cut to pieces that it was impossible for him to carry his equipment. His wife, a hardy Irishwoman, thereupon stepped forward, wrapped her husband up in his greatcoat and took her place in the column alongside him, carrying his jacket, knapsack and pouch on her own back.[8]

The tribulations of the Pullen family were of another nature. Mrs Pullen's husband, Richard, was a rifleman in the 95th with an unenviable reputation for trying to avoid foreign service. When his battalion was ordered to embark for the Peninsula in 1808, he managed to get himself excused on compassionate grounds on account of having a wife and two children, a boy and a girl named Charles and Susan. When the battalion had been abroad a short time, reinforcements were called for. As he was unable to produce an adequate excuse to win him further exemption he had to take his place in the draft. He arrived with his family in Spain in time to take part in Sir John Moore's campaign. The whole family took part in the retreat from Corunna and, during the first few days, it seemed improbable that any of them would manage to survive the incredible hardships of the march. On the very first day Pullen 'looked very chapfallen and seedy; and he was beginning even then to complain that he could not stand much more. The wife and children too were dropping behind.'[9] By the fourth day Pullen had become separated from his family. He continually bemoaned his fate, saying that he could stand no more and expected to fall dead

Wellington's triumphal entry into Madrid, 1812.

The battle of Fuentes d'Oñoro, 1811.

The French Army in retreat.

Sir William de Lancey.

Lady de Lancey.

The Duchess of Richmond's Ball, held on the eve of the battle of Quatre Bras in 1815.

The Duke of Wellington.

Wellington's troops leaving Brussels for the Waterloo campaign in 1815.

at any moment. In spite of this he managed, unlike many a better man, to struggle on to the coast and to get back to England.

In the meantime Mrs Pullen was having an even worse time. After being separated from her husband she lost both her children. She then joined up with a number of other women who had become detached from the column. Together they made their way as best they could towards the coast and the ships. In spite of the cold, the rain, the lack of food and the frightful conditions underfoot, somehow or other they managed to reach Corunna in time to embark with the army. This did not mean, however, that they had succeeded in escaping unscathed at the hands of the French soldiery. One night during a downpour the wretched women huddled into a barn for refuge. There they were discovered by French troops and savagely raped before being allowed to go on their way. Rifleman Harris describes the incident somewhat modestly by saying that they were 'overtaken by the French in the night, and treated by those gentlemen in a very unceremonious manner.'[10] In the case of Mrs Pullen her 'gentlemen's treatment' led to the birth of a son.

When he was safely installed in the transport which was to carry him to England, Pullen's comrades added to his depression by telling him that the best thing he could do was to reconcile himself to the fact that his family were all dead. In spite of this cheerless advice Pullen never gave up hope. From the moment he disembarked he spent all his time scouring the beaches, asking all and sundry if they had seen his wife and children. No one was able to give him any comfort until one day, to his amazement, he saw Mrs Pullen walking along the beach towards him. The two hobbled towards each other as quickly as their lacerated feet would allow, each hoping that the other would have news of the children. When they discovered that this was not the case, it was more than they could bear. They collapsed on the beach, sobbing bitterly.

When their grief had subsided and they had managed to pull themselves together, this otherwise rather feeble couple displayed great courage and tremendous tenacity in their attempts to recover their family. For days they made enquiries from everyone they met who had taken part in the retreat to see if they could get any clue as to what might have happened to the children. When these efforts produced no results they still did not give up hope but started advertising in the newspapers. In these endeavours they received little encouragement from their friends, who persisted in telling them that their children were undoubtedly lost and that they would be more sensible to give up their efforts and save their money. For a time it seemed that their friends were right, but in the end their persistence was rewarded. The artillery at Plymouth saw their advertisement and wrote to the Pullens to tell them that one night during the retreat they had heard a small girl crying on the mountainside. They had managed to collect her and had brought her back to England. The description of the child in the paper corresponded with the one they had found and they sent her on to Hythe. It was indeed their daughter Susan, who was overjoyed to be restored to her ecstatic parents.

Although Susan was recovered there was still no news of Charles, who was reluctantly given up for lost.

After these harrowing experiences Mrs Pullen had no desire for any further service abroad. When, to her dismay, in July 1809 the regiment was ordered to embark for Walcheren, she did her best to persuade her husband to avoid going, a course he was only too ready to follow. He tried to make himself appear unfit for service by rubbing snuff into his eyes so that they would look sore. But this rather pathetic subterfuge was easily detected and he was ordered to sail with his regiment in disgrace, without his wife and daughter. This proved to be his last taste of the active service he disliked so much. He caught the prevalent Walcheren fever and died. When the report of his death reached the rear party of his regiment at Hythe, Mrs Pullen was sent back to her parish in Warwickshire.

Some time after she had left, a letter arrived at Hythe from the boy Charles saying that he was a prisoner in France. The letter was opened by the bugle major who had not known Pullen and knew nothing of his story. By this time there were not very many men left at Hythe who had served with him and his company commander was dead. It seems that consequently no one took any interest in the letter and it was not forwarded to Mrs Pullen. As far as is known she never saw her son again.[11]

At first sight it seems strange that, even amongst the dangers and difficulties of the retreat, a mother should have allowed her children to have wandered out of her sight. But, under the conditions in which the army moved, the problems the women had to face in trying to keep their children constantly within reach must have been almost insoluble. Sergeant Donaldson tells of a young wife following in rear of the army, who sat down to suckle her baby. While she was doing this her little boy, aged about four, wandered off unnoticed. He walked back along the road towards the enemy. Before very long he found himself under heavy fire but was lucky enough to be saved from harm by a wounded French officer, who had been left behind by his regiment when it was driven back. The officer, who was badly hurt, wrapped the child in his greatcoat and sheltered him from danger by placing him in a ditch. After a little while two British soldiers passed by and the Frenchman asked them for something to drink. As they talked together the soldiers noticed the small boy. As he was dressed in the English style and told them his name was James, they realized that he was lost. They took possession of him and brought him back to their camp. A notice was then sent round the different divisions and in a few days the mother was reunited with her son.[12]

The devoted but less fortunate spouse of a badly-wounded sergeant of the 82nd followed her husband to the General Hospital at Fuenterrabia. She was appointed as nurse to the ward in which he was being treated. One day, when she was removing the bandage from an infected wound, she pricked her finger with a pin and caught the infection. To prevent the contagion from spreading her finger was removed. When this proved ineffective a second operation was performed to amputate her hand. When the infection again appeared she felt that she could stand no more and refused to undergo a further operation. The result was inevitable and she soon died.[13]

Though the brunt of the worry and work of looking after the children naturally fell on the long-suffering wives, the husbands were not entirely exempt. It may not, therefore, be out of place to close this chapter with one short tale of an unfortunate father. Towards the end of the campaign, when the army was well inside France, the wife of a soldier in the 94th Scots Brigade died, leaving her husband with a small child a few months old. He might well have looked round for some other woman to take care of the infant. Instead he elected to look after it himself. For some time, quite unaided, he did everything for his offspring. Day after day he was to be seen tramping along in the ranks with the little creature perched on top of his already heavy equipment. After a time he fell ill and was sent to hospital, taking the baby with him. He never rejoined his regiment and it is frustrating that we have no record of the eventual fate of this model father, and of the child he had looked after so conscientiously.[14]

Chapter

TEN

'THE PANGS OF DISPRISED LOVE'

THOUGH Wellington's marriage was a cold and unsuccessful
alliance, it was not because he was not fond of the ladies. On
the contrary, he admired pretty, witty women more than most men.
The story of his life is filled with a succession of female friends,
many of whom carried their feelings to the extent of adoration and
some of whom were adored in return. At the same time it is
impossible to avoid feeling that in these matters, as in all his
activities, his head was effectively in charge of his heart. He was not
a great romantic; every move was calculated. When he was told
that if a young major was not given leave his fiancée would die of a
broken heart, he wrote:

> We read, occasionally, of desperate cases of this description but I
> cannot say that I have ever yet known of a young lady dying of
> love. They contrive, in some manner, to live, and look tolerably
> well, notwithstanding their despair and the continued absence of
> their lover; and some have even been known to recover so far as
> to be inclined to take another lover, if the absence of the first has
> lasted too long. I don't suppose that your protegée can ever
> recover so far, but I do hope that she will survive the continued
> necessary absence of the Major, and enjoy with him hereafter
> many happy days.[1]

His great rival Napoleon's views on women and morals were
more basic and impulsive. According to him adultery was 'not by
any means a rare phenomenon but a very ordinary occurrence of
the sofa.' On the whole he thought that 'men treat women too well.
They have beauty, grace and the art of seduction; their obligations
should be dependence and subjection.'[2]

In spite of the opinions of these two great masters of war there were many ladies whose hearts did control their lives, even to the extent of dying of a broken heart. Though it might have been unusual for a British lady to carry her distress to this point, on the continent, where passions are apt to run higher, such tragedies did occur.

In the autumn of 1815 Private Wheeler was billeted in Verriers, a village about eight miles outside Paris. There he was quartered in the house of the Lebals, a poor old couple in their eighties, to whom the war had brought more than their fair share of tragedy and distress. Their family had originally consisted of six sons and one daughter. They were now childless. One son had been lost fighting in Italy, a second in Spain. Three more had died in the retreat from Moscow. When Napoleon was banished to Elba in May 1814, and a war-weary world started to look forward to an era of peace, only one boy remained to do the work for the Lebal family. Even he was not spared for long. Too soon the Corsican ogre returned to France, the armies of Europe were reformed, the struggle against Napoleon was renewed, and the sixth son perished at Waterloo. Not even the daughter was spared. She also was a victim of the war, for she gave her heart to a handsome face and a dashing uniform with tragic results. Wheeler tells us that 'she fell a victim to her pretended lover and shortly after died of a broken heart.'[3]

Early in his service in Portugal as a young medical officer, Dr Henry, whom we have already met as the admirer of Theodora and Donna Bernada, got involved in a case of attempted suicide. In May 1811 he had to call on Dr Bolton, a senior doctor from whom he was to receive his instructions. When his business was completed and he was about to take his leave, he was surprised to hear a long and piercing shriek, which clearly came from the upper storeys of the house. He was still more surprised when Dr Bolton, whose face had turned a chalky white, pushed past him and rushed for the door exclaiming, 'By God, she has killed herself.'

Dr Henry, left alone, was uncertain what he ought to do next. Should he make a tactful withdrawal, or should he remain and discover if Dr Bolton had been correct in his fears and a suicide had been attempted? He was not left in suspense for long. After a minute or so had elapsed a servant girl, who had nearly fallen down the stairs in her excitement, rushed into the room and asked him to come with her without delay. He went up the stairs and entered a bedroom where he found Dr Bolton and another maidservant attending an extremely attractive young woman, who was bleeding badly from her left breast. Dr Bolton was so upset that it was obvious he was not in a fit state to render his patient very effective aid. Nervous and shaken, he asked Dr Henry to attend to the wound. On examination Dr Henry discovered that the young woman had stabbed herself with a stiletto, but that serious damage had been avoided because the point of the weapon had struck a rib and had not made a very deep penetration of the chest. The hurt she had sustained was limited to what was little more than a flesh wound, the loss of some blood and, as the susceptible Henry was quick to notice, the piercing of a 'very white and well-formed bosom'. He had little trouble in stopping the bleeding, after which the would-be suicide was given restoratives, undressed and put to bed.

Dr Henry was then told that the young woman was a member of the Lisbon Opera Company. Dr Bolton had fallen for her charms and for some time she had been living with him. He had recently been recalled to England and had told the young lady that he proposed to end the liaison. This had very much upset her as she had hoped that he intended to marry her and take her home with him. A series of quarrels had come to a head on the morning of Dr Henry's visit. During a violent dispute Dr Bolton had lost his temper and abused the girl, calling her a 'fury and a fiend'. In despair she then told him that, if he would not take her with him, she would destroy herself and he would be responsible for her death. The stabbing incident was the sequel to this quarrel.

Unfortunately the story does not have a romantic ending. Dr Bolton refused to change his mind and left the country without the lady. Under the care of Dr Henry she was soon restored to good health and returned to the opera. Dr Henry rather ungallantly suspected that she had taken good care that the dagger should strike a rib and that she had no real intention of doing away with herself. Others may take a more sentimental view.[4]

One poor girl who *did* die of a broken heart was a nun in the convent of St Clara in Portalegre, where two convents were popular ports of call for officers billeted in the town. 'Dear nuns of Santa Clara! I thank thee for many an hour of nothingness; and thine, Santa Barbara, for many of a more intellectual cast' was the tribute of Kincaid's grateful pen. A regimental band frequently played in one or other of the convents' courtyards and officers would be invited into the convent parlour where they could talk to the nuns, though only through a double row of thick gratings. The sad story in question, which resulted from these meetings, is related by Sherer. He says:

> Some of these unfortunates were young and engaging: one, a very pretty, interesting girl, in the convent of Santa Clara, died before we left the city. She was passionately in love with a British officer, who was himself at the time much affected by her loss. I considered her death a mercy; for she must have either lived a life of hopeless misery, or dared to render asunder the sacred tie which bound her to her country, her family, and her convent, and have survived, perhaps, after all, the very flame to which she had so innocently given birth.[5]

In his letters home, Private Wheeler tells a story of another girl who nearly died from a broken heart, but this story did eventually have a happy ending. When he was in hospital in Fuenterrabia, he made friends with a French corporal who was able to speak English. While they were recovering from their wounds they had long talks from which Wheeler learned something of his friend Pipin's history. The Pipin family was well-to-do. Pipin himself was well educated and his father had planned that he should become an advocate. During his studies he had met and become engaged to a young woman. They were very much in love, never so happy as when they were together, and they intended to marry as soon as he was qualified. For some reason, which was never understood by Pipin, the young woman took umbrage at an imagined slight. To get her own back she embarked on a flirtation with another young man. Pipin was overcome with jealousy. He was quite unable to bear the sight of his beloved dallying with another. At the same time he was too proud to go to her and find out the cause of her coldness to him. At length he could stand it no longer. He ran away from home, went to Paris and enlisted.

His family heard no more of him until they got news that he had been wounded at the battle of Albuera, on 16 May 1811. They were then able to write and tell him that his running away had nearly caused the death of his sweetheart. When she heard that he had gone off to join the army, she had collapsed and for a long time was dangerously ill. After she recovered she took refuge in a convent declaring that, if Pipin did not return, she would spend the rest of her days in the shelter of its cloisters. As soon as Pipin's where-abouts were discovered the couple were quickly put in touch with each other again. Their vows to marry were renewed. Pipin told Wheeler that all he lived for was for the war to end so that he might go home and get wed.

When Napoleon was sent to Elba and hostilities temporarily came to an end, the two friends went back to their own countries and for a time lost touch with each other. Later, in December 1815 after taking part in the battle of Waterloo, Wheeler, who was in the army of occupation, found himself in Abbeville. As his regiment marched into the town, Pipin was standing in the crowd of onlookers. The two men spotted each other and at once resumed their former friendship. Wheeler was soon invited to the Pipin household, where he was delighted to meet the very happy Madame Pipin, who was about to present her spouse with their first offspring.[6]

Death from a broken heart is bad enough but it is at any rate final. There can be times when to go on living is an even sadder fate. So it was for Maria Josepha, whose tale must now be told. In 1811 the war in the Peninsula was in its third year. As its fortunes varied, the British and French armies advanced and retired. In the process, villages and farms were in the hands first of one side then of the other. This year it was the turn of the British to hold Fuentes d'Oñoro, a small town built on the side of a rocky ravine. At its foot runs a small stream and its narrow streets, which wind up the hill, are bounded on either side by stone walls. The grey stone, of which the village is built, is symbolic of the hard colourless life led by its inhabitants. Their houses were built of it and so was the little church, which still stands at the top of the ravine alongside the house of the curé. These two buildings, whose purpose was to bring peace and comfort to the village, were later in the year to become the centre of a murderous and bloody battle.

At the other end of the village, behind some pinewoods, lay a prosperous but lonely farm called the Quinta de Agila. Its owner was a well-to-do farmer, Camillo Siego by name. He had two sons, who helped him with the farm, and an outstandingly beautiful daughter, Maria Josepha.

When the British army arrived in the village Mr Augustus Schaumann, the cavalry commissary (*see* page 68), was billeted on the farm. He was lucky to get such good quarters, of the type which were usually allotted to general officers. The reason was that the farm contained some excellent stabling and storage space which the commissary department needed. Once he settled in, it was not difficult for him to ingratiate himself with the Siego family. He went out of his way to be pleasant to everyone, made himself useful about the house and, at a time when food was expensive and difficult to get, as a commissary he was able to supplement the family's larder and no doubt enrich it with small luxuries not generally obtainable. Secure in the good graces of the family, he was quick to make advances to Maria Josepha. He helped to draw water from the well. He sat by her side and told her amusing stories about England and Germany, which must have seemed like tales of another world to the simple, untravelled village girl. When he gave her a pair of Sheffield scissors to help her with her embroidery, the first use she made of them was to cut him a lock of her beautiful hair.

He had had much experience in gaining the confidence of women and Maria soon confessed to him how much she preferred the kindliness and good manners of the British officers to the loutish behaviour of the men of Fuentes d'Oñoro, and how much she dreaded the day when she would be forced to marry one of them. Under such circumstances it was not difficult for Mr Augustus, as he liked to be called, to win her love and complete his conquest. He was not very discreet about his success and later boasted that he was much envied by his friends. Strangely enough, at this time the affair seems to have gone unnoticed by the family.

On 5 May the French attacked the village in strength. Love-making was rudely interrupted. Maria Josepha and her family, accompanied by the village priest, fled from the village. Mr Augustus did what he could to help them on their way but he had little time to spare from his duties. During the battle the Quinta de Agila was badly damaged. When the fighting was over and the Siego family returned, they had to occupy another house in the middle of the village. Mr Augustus managed to pay them one brief visit before moving forward with his regiment.

During July he contracted malaria and at the beginning of August, while suffering from a sharp bout of fever, he was brought back to Fuentes and again lodged in the Quinta de Agila. One morning, as he lay in bed feeling far from well, he was brought a note from Maria Josepha, which contained the disquieting news that her father had ordained that she was to marry a well-known guerrilla leader. Utterly distraught, she implored Mr Augustus in the name of the Holy Family and all the saints to save her. Mr Augustus now began to realize that he was playing with fire. Camillo Siego was one of the most important men in the district. His house had on many occasions been used to accommodate very senior officers and he had recently received a commendatory letter from Wellington himself. Mr Augustus was well aware of the possible consequences of offending him. Even more alarming was the probable reaction of the Siego brothers and the guerrilla leader, all of whom were quite capable of making him pay for his dalliance with a knife or a bullet. Pondering these thoughts Mr Augustus hesitated, but it is much to his credit that, despite some trepidation, he overcame his fears and devised a plan.

Part of the house which Camillo now occupied was used as a bakery for the army. The bread was collected from the house and then distributed to the troops by Mr Augustus's muleteers. He instructed his head driver that, when he next went to the house, he was to smuggle a note to Maria Josepha. In this he told her that he would arrange to conceal two mules with their drivers in some ruins opposite her father's house. They would remain there each night until eleven o'clock ready to bring her to him. For the first two nights she found no opportunity to escape but on the third a load of wood was delivered to her father's yard. When the coachyard doors were opened to admit the wood, Maria escaped into the darkness. She ran to the mules and was quickly on her way to the Quinta and Mr Augustus's arms. She was not allowed to linger long. He sent her off as quickly as possible with two guards on fast mules to one of his friends in Portugal. As he had recently been promoted and was in funds, he was able to give her plenty of money to live on and to buy pretty clothes. He was, however, still extremely apprehensive. He therefore warned her and her escort to ride quickly and preserve the strictest secrecy. Then, with a last passionate kiss, she was off.

Mr Augustus's caution was wise. The next morning saw the arrival at the Quinta of a posse headed by Camillo. He was accompanied by his sons and some neighbours, all carrying firearms and knives, while one, who resembled Don Quixote, was equipped with a long lance. Camillo explained that as the Quinta was in need of extensive repairs it was necessary for him to make a thorough inspection of the whole building. Mr Augustus readily agreed. Thereupon every possible nook and cranny and all the rooms and outhouses were examined. Mr Augustus remained friendly and composed throughout the proceedings. When the search revealed nothing, the party prepared to depart. For a moment Mr Augustus thought that their suspicions had been allayed and that all would now be well. Unfortunately at this point some soldiers and muleteers, who were in the yard, began to laugh and mock Camillo. This, not unnaturally, infuriated him and he went off vowing vengeance. In spite of this setback Mr Augustus began to feel increasingly secure as the days passed and there was no further reaction. He was also immensely cheered by a letter from Maria Josepha telling him of her love and of how happy she was in her refuge.

A few days later, when he was beginning to congratulate himself that his plan had worked and the storm blown over, Mr Augustus received a summons to appear before the commissary-general. His fears revived and, sensing that he might be in serious trouble, he sent his friend, Mr Baldy, with a message that he was unable to come as he had a high fever. This subterfuge did him no good at all. Mr Baldy was closely examined and, when he tried to prevaricate, the commissary-general cut the ground from under his feet by suddenly producing the escape note, which Maria Josepha had unwisely failed to destroy and which had been discovered by her father. Camillo had complained to Lord Wellington, who had expressed his annoyance and given orders that Maria Josepha was to be returned to her parents forthwith.

This was too much for Mr Augustus who surrendered without further ado. He put as good a face on the affair as he could by explaining to Camillo that his intentions were strictly honourable and that he was merely trying to save Maria Josepha from an unhappy marriage. She would return to her family as pure as when she left it. This likely tale was accepted by Camillo, who promised that he would neither punish her on her return nor force her to marry the guerrilla.

When Maria Josepha was collected by her parents, she was almost out of her mind with grief. She refused to eat, would not speak to anyone and spent her days weeping in her mother's arms. Camillo added to her misery by seizing all the pretty clothes that Mr Augustus had bought for her and chopping them into small pieces, which he burnt on the kitchen fire. She made two further attempts to escape to her lover but on each occasion was caught by her brothers and dragged home. It may be unkind but one suspects that she would not have been received with much enthusiasm if her escapes had been successful. By this time Mr Augustus's feet were cold even if his heart was still warm. Though he remained in the area for some time he made no further effort to visit her.

He never saw her again but, one day, when he was far away at the foot of the Pyrenees, he had news of her. He was warming himself by the fireside of an inn when he met some girls from Fuentes who had married British soldiers and had marched across Spain with the army. They told him that she still pined for him, ate little and spent a listless, unhappy life, wandering aimlessly through the rooms of the Quinta. Mr Augustus had the grace to shed a few tears.

At the end of 1812 Harry Smith of the 95th was stationed in Fuentes and lived with his wife in Camillo's house. They took a great fancy to their host and considered that he and his family had been infamously treated by Mr Augustus. They were much distressed at seeing their poor girl in such an unhappy state. Her dejected manner and vacant looks seemed to them a sign that she was almost out of her mind. Juana Smith, with the help of the priest, did what she could to raise her spirits but Maria's heart was not to be mended. She lived and died sorrowing for her lost lover.[7]

ELEVEN

LADY DE LANCEY

TO lose a husband by death on the battlefield is a catastrophe and a shock, but the blow, though sudden, is decisive. The pangs of suspense can be just as painful and even more exhausting. To be told that one's husband has come through a great battle unharmed, then to hear that he is dead; to give way to despair and to be roused from the depths of grief to learn that he is alive but desperately wounded; to make a dash to the battlefield to see that he is properly cared for, to be greeted by the doctors with encouraging reports, to see him grow steadily weaker and finally to watch him die, is a strain more prolonged and painful than a young bride should have to undergo. Such was the fate of Lady Magdalene de Lancey.

On 4 April 1815 Magdalene Hall, the daughter of Sir James Hall of Dunglass, married Colonel Sir William de Lancey. The young couple were deeply in love, their circumstances were comfortable and in normal times they should have been able to look forward to a long and happy life together. These, however, were not normal times. They were overshadowed by the escape of Napoleon from Elba and the prospect of war. Within a fortnight of the wedding Sir William was on his way to Brussels to take up the appointment of quartermaster-general on the Duke of Wellington's staff.

The appointment was unexpected. When Lord Wellington assumed command of the allied army it already had a quartermaster-general. The appointment was held by Sir Hudson Lowe, an officer whom the Duke disliked. He described him to Creevey, the Whig politician whose journal *The Creevey Papers* has provided an important contribution to the social history of the period, in no uncertain terms:

As for Lowe, he is a damned fool. When I came to Brussels from Vienna in 1815, I found him quartermaster-general of the army here, and I presently found the damned fellow would instruct me in the equipment of the army, always producing the Prussians to me as models; so I was obliged to tell him that I had commanded a much larger army in the field than any Prussian general, and that I was not to learn from their service how to equip an army. I thought this would have stopped him, but shortly afterwards the damned fellow was at me again about the equipment of the Prussians; so I was obliged to write home and complain of him, and the Government was kind enough to take him away from me.[1]

It was this that led to Magdalene's troubles for, when Lowe was posted away, de Lancey, who had served on the QMG's staff in the Peninsula, was sent out at the Duke's request as the replacement.

Magdalene did not accompany him on his journey to the continent but followed as soon as he was able to make satisfactory arrangements for her accommodation. She disembarked at Ostend on 8 June and immediately took the road for Brussels. As she drove through the countryside, although she knew that on all sides the allied armies were concentrating for a new outbreak of war, she was amazed at the peaceful atmosphere which seemed to permeate the scene.

When she arrived at the capital she was delighted with the quarters that had been found for her. They consisted of a comfortable suite of rooms in a house situated in the park and belonging to Count de Lannoy. She was charmed with her host who received his new guests with great kindness and cordiality. Her joy at being reunited with her husband was only dimmed by one nagging fear. William told her that with any luck they should have at least a month together before any fighting broke out, but she could not help being worried that he was too sanguine. She feared that the time might be all too short before they were separated again.

For this reason, though Brussels was at the time a lively centre of social activity, she declined the many invitations to balls, concerts and other amusements that were showered on them. She and William preferred to stay at home and share each other's company. The Duchess of Richmond's famous ball was but one of the many events to which they were bidden but did not go in order that they might spend the evening alone together.

Nevertheless, the life they led, though simple and quiet, was in Magdalene's view the most blissful period of her existence. Sir William, who surprisingly does not seem to have been over-burdened by work, was seldom called upon to spend more than an hour in his office during the day, which left him plenty of time to devote to his bride. Their routine was regular. In the afternoons they went for walks together, rarely meeting anyone as the fashionable hour for dinner was between three and four. They had their own meal at six and it was customary for William to invite two or three of his friends whom he wished Magdalene to meet, to join them.

Naturally they discussed what Magdalene was to do when hostilities broke out and William had to leave for the front. Magdalene would have liked to follow the army but William did not wish her to undergo the rigours and hardships of what might develop into a long and dangerous campaign. It was decided that Antwerp was the most suitable place for her to shelter. It was strongly fortified, not too far from Brussels and, should the worst come to the worst, was a port from which an escape to England could easily be effected.

On the afternoon of 15 June de Lancey broke his normal rule and, for the first time since Magdalene arrived in Brussels, accepted an invitation. He went to dine with Alava, the Spanish plenipotentiary and a great friend of Wellington's. When he had been away about half an hour, an aide-de-camp arrived at the house asking for him. On being told that he was with Alava, the ADC remounted and set off at full gallop. A few minutes later Magdalene, who was watching from her window, began to feel alarmed when she saw her husband ride past their house and dismount at the Duke of Wellington's residence, which was a short distance further on. Her fears increased when she saw William jump from the saddle and hurry into the Duke's house, leaving his horse unattended in the middle of the road.

He did not return until nine in the evening, when, seeing that Magdalene was very upset, his first thought was to comfort her and allay her fears. He then told her that a great battle was expected and that she must be ready to leave for Antwerp at six o'clock the following morning. His immediate task was to set about writing the orders for the movement of the troops. He asked her to prepare some strong green tea which would help to sustain him as he worked through the night. For some time, as he went on with his writing, messengers kept arriving at the house to collect the orders for their divisions. Occasionally he had to interrupt his work to visit his office or go to the Duke.* On one of these visits he found the latter, garbed in shirt tails and slippers, half dressed for the Richmond ball, poring over a map with Baron Muffling who, by contrast, was fully clothed in full-dress uniform complete with orders and decorations.

De Lancey returned from this incongruous scene to continue writing his orders. The Duke, on the other hand, went off to attend the ball where he would be in contact with most of the senior British and allied officers. His appearance at the ball was clearly a well-calculated act and far from the frivolous move that is sometimes suggested. It should be added that the Duke was back in bed and fast asleep at two a.m. and up at five-thirty a.m., feeling perfectly fresh.

At three a.m. William and Magdalene, looking out of their window, saw the troops assembling in the park. Mrs Eaton, the authoress of *Waterloo Days*, who was staying in Brussels at the time with her brother, has left a moving description of the regiments forming up while the men said a fond farewell to their families:

> Numbers were taking leave of their wives and children, perhaps for the last time, and many a veteran's rough cheek was wet with tears of sorrow. One poor fellow, immediately under our windows, turned back again and again to bid his wife farewell, and take his baby once more in his arms; and I saw him hastily brush away a tear with the sleeve of his coat as he gave her back the child for the last time, wrung her hand, and ran off to join his company, which was drawn up on the other side of the Place Royale. Many of the soldiers' wives marched out with their husbands to the field, and I saw one young English lady slowly

---

* It is sometimes said that the Duke was caught unprepared by Napoleon's rapid advance. It is, however, beyond doubt that he was well aware that something was afoot since he told Lady Salisbury that from 13 to 15 June he was always to be found within twenty yards of his home in Brussels.[2]

riding out of the town along with an officer, who, no doubt, was her husband.[3]

The time for the de Lanceys' own parting was soon upon them. At six a.m. Magdalene left for Antwerp. Before she left, William gave her a letter addressed to Captain Mitchell, who was serving there in the QMG's department, asking him to look after her and give her all the help he could.

Soon after her arrival she was installed in a comfortable inn. As her room was at the back of the house she was sheltered from the considerable noise and confusion that filled the busy streets. Because she had been warned that the town would be full of rumours and tittle-tattle which she did not wish to hear, she remained confined in her room and did not wander out or pay any visits. Her maid, Emma, attended to her wants and Captain Mitchell kept her in touch with what was going on. At midnight on the 17th she was greatly relieved to get a note from William telling her that a battle had been fought at Quatre Bras and that he was unharmed. Emma, on the other hand, was much alarmed. On her expeditions to the shops she had seen numbers of wounded men being brought into the town and had heard that many of the English ladies were departing for England without further delay. She wondered if they would be wise to do the same. Magdalene, who would not hear of such a scheme, offered to let her sail for home, if she felt so inclined, but Emma at once indignantly repudiated any suggestion that she should desert her mistress.

On 18 June the great battle was fought. Early in the morning Lieutenant Gronow of the 1st Foot Guards saw Wellington and his staff riding forward from their headquarters to the battlefield. De Lancey was amongst them and 'they all seemed as gay and unconcerned as if they were riding to meet the hounds in some quiet English county'.[4] As the day went by it became painfully clear that, in fact, the perils of war vastly exceed those of the hunting field. Wellington's staff suffered its full share of casualties. The Duke himself, who throughout the day was under the hottest fire and escaped unscathed, had good reson to reflect that 'the hand of Almighty God has been upon me this day'. De Lancey was not so lucky. About four p.m., just before the first of the great French cavalry attacks, he was knocked off his horse and carried several yards through the air by the blast of a cannon ball. At first he was thought to be dead but, when it appeared that he was still alive and had some chance of recovery, his cousin, Lieutenant-Colonel Delancey Barclay of the 1st Foot Guards, arranged for him to be wrapped in a blanket and carried to a barn in the farm of Mont St Jean, about half a mile away. Later, when it was feared that the barn might be taken by the enemy, he was moved to a cottage near the village of Waterloo. There he was left unattended during the whole of the night and part of the following day. He was then discovered by an officer of the staff corps and proper arrangements made for his care and treatment. This neglect of a senior staff officer may seem reprehensible but, though it is true that many of the wounded were unfortunately not attended to until days after the battle, it should not be thought that the arrangements for caring for them were heartless and haphazard or below the standards of the time. On the contrary, Tomkinson, an officer in the 16th Light Dragoons, records that 'many surgeons came from England for the practice, and on things being arranged, no wounded could be better attended to. The wounded of the British army generally receive more attention than those of other nations.'[5] And a sergeant-major, who was also present at the battle, says that 'a number of poor fellows, who were carried to the houses of the neighbouring villages, met with the most humane treatment; many there breathed their last, under circumstances less appalling than on the battlefield.'[6]

On the morning after the battle Captain Mitchell called on Magdalene to give her the splendid news that a great battle had been fought, that the French were utterly routed and that there would be no further fighting. Best of all her husband was safe and unhurt. When asked if he was certain of this he was able to reassure her that he had seen the list of killed and wounded and that Sir William's name was not on it. It was then that Magdalene began to realize how great her anxiety had been. For two hours she paced up and down her room in a fever of relief, trying to unwind her pent-up nerves. While she was thus engaged she was told that a Lady Hamilton, the wife of Sir Hew Hamilton who was staying in Antwerp, was in the inn parlour and wished to speak to her. When she went downstairs she found Lady Hamilton in a highly emotional state. She was obviously overwrought, but Magdalene attributed her odd manner to the effect on her nerves of the very heavy casualties the army had suffered on the previous day. After some desultory remarks Lady Hamilton enquired if Magdalene had actually heard from her husband, to which she replied that, though she had not actually had a letter from him, she had seen the casualty list and knew that he was unhurt. After some hesitation Lady Hamilton confessed that the casualty list had been compiled by her from information given to her by a general who had been at the battle. She had, however, omitted a number of names to avoid giving pain to relatives who were still in Antwerp. One of the names she had left out was Sir William's.

Magdalene's joy was at once turned to horror. She immediately jumped to the conclusion that her husband had been killed and it was only with the greatest difficulty that Lady Hamilton could stop her uncontrollable sobbing and reassure her that he was still alive, though desperately wounded. As soon as she realized that there was still a chance of seeing him alive, Magdalene decided that she must leave for Brussels with as little delay as possible. While her carriage was being prepared and horses obtained, Captain Mitchell ordered an officer to gallop to Brussels and discover exactly where William was to be found. He was then to return as quickly as possible so that he could meet Magdalene on the road and give her the latest news.

The two hours that it took to complete the preparations for her journey to Brussels seemed interminable to Magdalene. She was nearly mad with worry, which was aggravated by the knowledge that, if Lady Hamilton had not interfered with the casualty lists, she would already have been well on her way. At long last she and Emma set out on their dismal journey. At first their progress was agonizingly slow. The gates out of Antwerp were almost impassable as the roads were blocked by the 'crowd of waggons, carts and horses, wounded men, deserters or runaways and all the rabble and confusion resulting from the previous three days' fighting'.

Just before the carriage reached Malines it was approached by an officer. The coachman, recognizing him as Mr William Hay of the 16th Light Dragoons, pulled up. Magdalene lowered the window and, on enquiring if he had any news of her husband, received the dreadful reply, 'I fear I have very bad news for you, it is all over.' Her hopes completely destroyed by this one dreadful sentence, Magdalene virtually collapsed. In a state of acute misery and hardly knowing what to do, she ordered the coachman to turn round and return to Antwerp.

When she was back in her inn and had had time to recover her wits, she began to wonder if Mr Hay was absolutely certain that William was dead. She sent him a message asking him to call on her. When he arrived she asked him if he was quite sure of what he had said. He could give her little comfort. He reported that he had not been engaged in the fighting himself and was not near Sir William when he was hit. He had, however, been given reliable information that he had been knocked from his horse by a cannon ball and that the Duke was with him when he died.

Mr Hay seemed so certain that Magdalene was persuaded that there could be no further hope. In her distress she locked herself in her room, refused to see any visitors and decided that her only course was to return to England. Emma, who was much alarmed by her manner, consulted her friends, who advised that a doctor should be sent for to bleed her. Magdalene refused to submit to any treatment but she did allow Emma, who by this time had begun to fear for her mistress's sanity as well as her health, to move her bed into her room and remain with her during the night. The next day, when visitors attempted to see her, Emma was ordered to turn them away and keep the door locked. At length one determined caller arrived who was not to be put off. After a lengthy conversation through the door Emma came to her mistress's bedside to tell her that General McKenzie, the commander of the Antwerp garrison, was below with certain information that de Lancey was alive and that there were hopes of his recovery. Re-inspired by this extraordinary news Magdalene rushed downstairs to see the general. By this time she was so distraught that she did not know what she could believe and her first words to the general were to warn him that it would be too cruel to buoy her up with false hopes. He replied that he would not think of doing such a thing and he was soon able to persuade her that his information was undoubtedly correct.

Having succeeded in allaying her near hysteria, General McKenzie showed her the greatest kindness. He arranged for horses to draw her carriage from Antwerp to Brussels and sent a dragoon forward to arrange for a change of horses to be ready to take her on to Waterloo when she arrived in the capital. With this help it was not long before she was on the road again. The congestion was less than it had been on the previous day though the road was still crowded and many of the travellers on it were suffering from frayed tempers. When the carriage attempted to pass a slow-moving army wagon, a German officer drew his sword in a rage and endeavoured to strike first the coachman then the horses. A personal appeal from Magdalene herself was necessary to calm him down.

Just as they were entering Brussels they again met Mr Hay, who had returned from Antwerp to search for his missing brother. He had found out where Sir William was housed and was also able to guide Magdalene's carriage to the spot where the fresh horses were waiting. As soon as they had been harnessed to the carriage Magdalene continued her journey, Mr Hay, his sword drawn, riding in front as an escort. Owing to the large number of vehicles, animals and pedestrians in the overcrowded road, the nine miles' drive took three and a half long hours, each filled with worry and apprehension for Magdalene.

When they arrived at the broken-down little cottage where William was in bed, Magdalene was met by Sir George Scovell, an officer on his staff. Sir George warned her that William was in a very precarious state and that, however anxious about him she might be, it was essential that she should appear calm and confident. He then took her in to see her husband. She found him in a dingy little room with no furniture except his bed and one broken chair. The bed was no more than a rough wooden frame fastened to the wall. Though she was dismayed by the discomfort of William's surroundings she was pleased and surprised at the strength of his voice, and by hearing him talk of how much he looked forward to his convalescence and being with her. As soon as they had finished greeting each other, Magdalene set about making him more comfortable. His pillow, made of a bag of dusty chaff which made him cough, was replaced by a cushion from the carriage; the bedclothes were scrapped and exchanged for a new blanket and clean sheets.

Possibly to keep up her spirits, the doctors' first reports were encouraging. They said that, if they could keep the fever at bay, there were no other alarming symptoms and there was a good chance of recovery. To keep his temperature down they resorted to constant bleeding. After the first day or two Magdalene, in spite of their reassuring words, could see from their expressions that they knew William had no chance of getting better. She managed to master her unhappiness in an effort to make his last days as happy as possible. She hardly ever left his side and got practically no sleep.

A number of ingenious devices were employed to make his life more tolerable. She found that he was very fond of cups of tea but that it was very difficult to buy milk. This problem was overcome by the soldier servant, who discovered that an accommodating Prussian cow was tethered nearby. From that moment it became one of the duties of this convenient animal to provide large jugs of milk for the patient. The air in the ill-ventilated room was stale and unpleasant. It was found that the smoke rising from vinegar and burning charcoal made the room seem much fresher.

Magdalene told Emma that she must not allow visitors into the cottage as William found them exhausting. A special exception was naturally made when the Duke of Wellington called. This visit was a great success, the warmth of the Duke's manner doing much to cheer William up. Otherwise he saw practically no one except Dr Powell, his doctor. It is an extraordinary fact that this overworked medico had to do all his visiting on his own feet though there were still wounded to be attended to lying out in the fields, among the dead. It is little wonder that he confessed to Magdalene that he 'was sometimes quite knocked up with walking many miles on the heavy road to the fields and cottages.'

On 24 June the bruise on William's side became very painful, and a messenger was sent to Brussels for leeches. When they arrived it was found that Magdalene, who had no previous experience, was more skilful in applying them than the surgeon. He was delighted at her aptitude and was only too pleased to pass this duty over to her in view of his own fatigue. On the same day as the leeches were obtained Dr Hume, the Duke's physician, came to see the patient. Though he meant well and tried to cheer William up, Magdalene thought his manner a great deal too jovial and was not at all sorry when he took his departure.

The next day William was worse. Mr Woolriche, an excellent doctor and a deputy-inspector of the medical department, was summoned. Despite his efforts and frequent visits he could do little to help. William's condition continued to deteriorate until, by the evening of the 26th, it was clear that he had only hours rather than days left. Magdalene therefore sent a note to General Dundas, his great friend, telling how desperate the case was. The general kindly made immediate arrangements to come to Waterloo to support her.

Dr Hume then advised that further poultices should be applied. Though these did something to relieve William's suffering, it was all too clear that they could be no more than palliatives. He lingered on a few more hours before dying in some pain. The two doctors, Hume and Powell, were in attendance. His wife was by his side.

General Dundas took Magdalene back to her old room in Count de Lannoy's house in Brussels. De Lancey's body was brought back for burial in a Protestant cemetery alongside many others who had fallen in the battle. Immediately after the funeral Magdalene returned to England 'in a violence of grief more like a delirium than the sorrow of a Christian'. Their marriage had lasted just over three months and Magdalene later wrote that she had never forgotten 'the perfection of her happiness while it lasted'.

Some time after these events Magdalene wrote an account of her experiences, *A Week at Waterloo*. A copy found its way into the hands of Charles Dickens and Walter Scott, two of the great novelists of the day. Scott said, 'I have never read anything that affected my feelings more strongly.' Dickens went further and wrote, 'If I live for fifty years, I shall dream of it every now and then, from this hour to the day of my death.' There can be little doubt that had Magdalene been a character in a novel of the time she would, after such a devastating experience, have gone into a decline and speedily followed her husband to the grave. She was, however, a real person and therefore more resilient. Two years later she married Captain Henry Harvey of the Madras infantry, by whom she had a child. The ultimate tragedy is that she did not enjoy her new-found happiness for long. She died in 1822.

(This chapter is mainly based on *A Week at Waterloo* and the quotations are taken from that work.)

EPILOGUE

THIS book has concentrated on the women who accompanied Wellington's army, but his were not the only wars in which women followed the drum. In earlier days some had even succeeded in masquerading as men in order to enlist in the forces. Of these the best known were Christian Davies and Phoebe Hessell.

Christian Davies was born in Dublin in 1667, the daughter of a brewer. At the age of seventeen she was seduced by her cousin who later became a clergyman. She then went to live with her aunt, an innkeeper who, when she died, left Christian all her property. Christian carried on the business and married one of the waiters. This cannot have been a great success as he later ran away, though he did let her know that he had joined the army and was in Flanders fighting the French. She decided to go and find him and succeeded in getting to the war by enlisting in an infantry regiment. There she was wounded and taken prisoner but, after being exchanged for an enemy prisoner, rejoined the army as a trooper in the 2nd Dragoons (Scots Greys). She returned to England after the Treaty of Ryswick (1697) had been signed, but on the outbreak of the War of the Spanish Succession (1703) she returned to Flanders with the 2nd Dragoons and fought in a number of engagements under Marlborough, including the battle of Blenheim where she at last found her husband. However, by this time she was so keen on leading the life of a trooper that she swore him to secrecy. Two years later she was badly wounded at Ramillies (1706). Her true sex was then discovered and she was dismissed from the service. She then resumed female attire and remained at the war with her husband as his wife. After he was killed at Malplaquet (1709) she made two further ventures into matrimony and when she died in 1739 was buried among the Chelsea Pensioners.

Phoebe Hessell, though an old woman, was still alive when Wellington's army was ploughing its way backwards and forwards across the Peninsula but not too old to study the war news as she sat in her house by the sea. She did not need to call on her imagination when she read the accounts of the battles. She had been a soldier herself. She was born in Stepney in 1713 in the reign of good Queen Anne. When she grew up she too managed to conceal her sex and enlisted in the 5th Regiment of Foot. In the War of the Austrian Succession (1740–1748) she served with her regiment until 1745 when she was wounded at the battle of Fontenoy. The doctor who attended her discovered that she was a woman and she was sent back to England. Many of those she now read about would never return to tell the tale. She had been luckier. War had done nothing to shorten her life. She was 102 in the year of Waterloo and she lived for a further six years. She spent her old age in Brighton where she was able to live in reasonable comfort with the help of a small pension she received from the Prince Regent. She was buried in Brighton but by 1850 her tombstone had fallen into disrepair. A subscription list was started to put it in order and it is a fitting postscript to her story to record that the Duke of Wellington was one of those who gave money for the restoration of the grave, which is still well preserved in St Nicholas's churchyard, Brighton.

After Waterloo there was a period of peace but soldiers' wives still continued to be taken abroad to their husbands' peacetime stations. Thus there were many such wives in India, and January 1842 found Lady Sale, the wife of General Sir Robert Sale, in Kabul with her daughter and son-in-law, Lieutenant Sturt of the engineers. In January of that year the Afghan tribes rose in revolt against their British imposed ruler. The British garrison of Kabul was withdrawn under promise of safe conduct but was treacherously ambushed and massacred in the Khoord Kabul Pass. Lady Sale was twice slightly wounded and her clothes were said to be riddled with bullets. Her son-in-law was killed but she, her daughter and other women were taken into captivity. Though not maltreated they spent a miserable time in overcrowded accommodation with no spare clothes and only the roughest of food. Under these conditions Mrs Sturt gave birth to a daughter. After being herded from one fastness to another, they were eventually rescued by Sir Richard Shakespeare at the head of six hundred tribal horsemen. When Mrs Sturt's husband died in 1845, Queen Victoria granted her a pension of £500 a year in recognition of her bravery and her services.

The Crimean War (1854–56) saw the end of the ballot system for taking wives abroad and was the last campaign in which they accompanied their husbands to war. Even before the war started there had been an agitation to better the lot of the soldiers' wives, both at home and abroad, and, though this had produced no immediate results, when the scandals of the maladministration of the war became public, it did lead to far-reaching improvements. When war was declared the British army had not been engaged with a European enemy for fifty years and the administrative services, which had been neglected during the long years of peace, were incapable of dealing with the problems of a major war. The sufferings of the women were intense. On the way out some were put ashore at Scutari and accommodated in rat-infested shelters under some old Turkish barracks. At Varna, a primitive Black Sea port which was selected as a staging post for the operations, there was a shortage of water and the sanitary arrangements were so bad that epidemics of dysentery and cholera broke out. Even so, when the army was due to sail on the Crimea, the hundreds of wives who had accompanied it so far were at first forbidden to follow. As they had neither money, food nor housing this unreasonable order had to be cancelled and they were then crowded on to the already over-congested troopships. In the Crimea itself conditions were no better. However, out of all this misery good was to come. For the first, time news from a battle area was fully reported in the home press and the tales of the suffering of the soldiers and their wives became public property. The redoubtable Florence Nightingale, who was sent out to organize and supervise the nursing staff, added her voice to the need for reforms. A Commission appointed by the government confirmed the truth of the complaints. All this had an effect on public opinion and the government. When the war was over, the conditions under which soldiers and their wives were expected to live in peacetime were also examined, and found to be thoroughly unhealthy. Florence Nightingale pronounced the effective dictum that 'our soldiers enlist to death in the barracks'. Since then there has been a continual stream of improvements. The army wife has received the recognition that is her due. Unless there are operational reasons to prevent it she accompanies her husband whenever he is overseas. She is allotted married quarters at home and abroad. She now travels by air but, even before the days of the troopships were over, she no longer had to make her journey in an overcrowded, unhealthy ship, sleeping on the same decks as the men, but cruised in a well-found, modern vessel. The conduct of the Crimean War was not something of which the nation can be proud, but at least it was largely responsible for the excellent conditions which the modern army wife enjoys.

In spite of all these improvements would it be too cynical to wonder if, in their own brave, rough, undemanding way, Mrs Anton, Mrs Reston, Mrs Howans and their sisters were not just as happy and contented with their lot?

APPENDICES

A

When a Regiment embarks for active Field Service, the number of Soldiers' Wives to be permitted to accompany it must be limited to Six per Company, or their embarkation must be altogether forbidden, according to the nature of the Service for which the Regiment may be destined.

To such wives of Soldiers as are not permitted to embark with their Husbands, the Rates of Allowance, authorized by the Act of the 51st of George III., chap 120, will be granted, to enable them to proceed to their Homes, or to the Places at which they intend to reside, during the absence of their Husbands on Service.

Regulations and Orders for the Army, 1811

B

Medellin, 23 August 1809

1 Officers commanding divisions and brigades, will be pleased to take measures to prevent the women, and followers of the army, from buying up the bread which is prepared for the soldiers' rations. This practice, carried on in the irregular manner it is at present, must ultimately prejudice the soldiers, and prevent the regular supply of bread.

2 The women of the army must be prevented from purchasing bread in the villages, within two leagues of the station of any division of the army: when any woman wants to purchase bread, she must ask the Officer of the company to which she belongs, for a passport, which must be countersigned by the commanding officer of the regiment. Any woman found with bread in her possession, purchased at any place nearer than two leagues, will be deprived of the bread by the provost or his assistants; as will any woman who goes out of camp to purchase bread without a passport. Women, who will have been discovered disobeying the order, will not be allowed to receive rations.

The Duke of Wellington's General Orders

C

Badajoz, 1 October 1809

1 The commander of the forces observes that the women of the regiments have come up from Lisbon along with the clothing, to the great inconvenience of the army and to their own detriment: and as they travel on the cars, they delay and render uncertain the arrival of the regimental clothing for the troops, and defeat all arrangements for bringing it up to the army.

2 The commander of the forces desires that Colonel Peacocke will prevent the women from leaving Lisbon, with the clothing and regimental baggage; and the officers and non-commissioned officers coming up from Lisbon, in charge of clothing, are desired to prevent the women from travelling on the carts.

The Duke of Wellington's General Orders

D

War Office, 20 August 1810

My Lord

I have the honour to acquaint your Lordship that His Majesty has been pleased to direct that the same allowances shall be made to the widows and children of soldiers dying abroad, and sent home in consequence thereof, as are granted to the wives and children of soldiers embarking for foreign service.

To entitle people to the allowances in question, it will be necessary that they should produce certificates from the commanding officer of the corps in which their husbands or fathers (as the case may be) died abroad, and that they are therefore sent home.

(Signed) Palmerston

Letter from the secretary at war to the commander of the forces

Frenada, 8 December 1811
The following letter from the secretary of His Royal Highness the commander-in-chief, is published for the information of the army.

Horse Guards, 5 November 1811
My Lord
In order to establish a general system in the issue of provisions to the wives and children of soldiers on foreign stations, the commander-in-chief, in concurrence with the Lords Commissioners of His Majesty's Treasury, has been pleased to approve of the following regulations, and to desire that they may be strictly attended to in all issues made to the troops under your command:

i That rations shall not be issued to women and children of regiments in the field, in a greater proportion than six women and their children per troop or company; and to women and children in a stationary garrison, in a greater proportion than twelve women and their children of each troop or company.

ii Women and children of Royal Veteran Battalions are to be victualled to the full number which may be in the regiment.

iii Widows and orphans of officers or soldiers are to be victualled until they can obtain a passage home.

iv No women or children, except the wives and children of non-commissined officers and privates, shall be entitled to rations except as aforesaid.

v The rations for each woman shall be one half, of each child one third, of that allowed to a man.

vi The women and children to be victualled, in pursuance of these regulations, to be nominated by the commanding officer of the corps; and their names to be specially returned to the commissary.

I have the honour to be (etc)
H. Torrens

The Duke of Wellington's General Orders

Badajoz, 12 September 1809
The women and children of the officers and soldiers of the army are entitled, the former each to half a ration, the latter to a quarter of a

ration daily; and I see no objection to extending these allowances to the wives and children of clerks and others employed in the public departments, provided they are English born. If the clerk be Portuguese, it may be necessary and proper to give him his rations, but it cannot be necessary to his wife and children, and I desire that this practice be discontinued.

I conclude that the rations drawn by the lady to whom you refer as an officer's wife, are for the wives of other officers or soldiers, and if so they are perfectly regular; if not, they must be discontinued; and, at all events, forage must not be allowed to the horse of an officer's lady residing at Lisbon.

I beg that you will understand that I am desirous of giving to the wives of the officers and soldiers of the army every indulgence to the fullest extent allowed by His Majesty's regulations; but I can suffer no abuse, and every appearance of abuse must be checked immediately.

The officers of the army are allowed to draw rations in the field for servants not soldiers, paying for the same; and I conceive the same indulgence may be extended to their families residing at Lisbon for English servants, but not for Portuguese.

Letter from the commander of the forces to the
administrative commandant in Lisbon

F

Adjutant-General's Office, Toulouse, 26 April 1814
Sir
The embarkation of the British army being one of the first consequences to be expected from the successful campaign, I am desired by the commander of the forces to suggest to you the expediency of attempting an arrangement in behalf of the Portuguese and Spanish women, followers of the army, to enable their return to their respective homes.

It is natural that this description of women should not determine on separating from those with whom they have lived till urged to do so, yet timely decision seems to be the only means of avoiding eventual distress.

Although the field marshal foresees the necessity of leaving the greater number of the foreign women behind, who with reasonable provision may accompany the Portuguese troops to the rear; yet I am to observe, there will be no objection to a few of those who have proved themselves useful and regular, accompanying the soldiers to whom they are attached, with a view to their being ultimately married: it will appear evident to you, however, that from the unsettled life and habits of followers of the army, such selection should be made with the greatest caution.

I have to beg you will inform me of the plan you propose adopting and the number of women who are to come under its influence; and mention if you conceive that any other general arrangement will answer better than that to which I have alluded.

Officers commanding regiments who have allowed women to follow their corps, with the power to limit that indulgence, should certainly take an interest in providing for their decent departure.

I have the honour to be, Sir
Your very obedient servant,
E.M. Packenham, A.G.
A circular letter to general officers commanding divisions

G

Cuellar, 1 August 1812
The followers of the army, the Portuguese women in particular, must be prevented by the provosts from plundering the gardens and fields of vegetables. The women must be informed that they must obey orders, or they will be turned out of the army.
The Duke of Wellington's General Orders

H

Cadiz, 29 December 1812
In regard to the ladies, they have certainly no right to be lodged in billets, but it would be cruel to deprive them of that accommodation. I do not believe I can authorize their having this advantage by an order, and the point can be settled only in communication with the government. If the matter could be allowed to go on, as it is

now, I would write a letter to Peacocke to be circulated among the ladies which would give them a little advice on the subject, and make them better behaved.

Extract from a letter from the commander of the forces to Marshal Beresford

I

St Jean de Luz, 12 January 1814

I have the honour of receiving your letter of 24 December, to which I should have replied at an earlier date if I had not been engaged with the operations of the army, and I assure you that I feel the utmost concern that you should conceive that you have any reason to complain of any of the persons attached to the British army.

There can be no doubt that no person can have a right to claim quarters in any town to which he is not obliged to go on duty, or by wounds or sickness acquired in the service; and the grant of quarters to ladies, the wives of officers of the army, can be considered in no other light than as an indulgence.

I should not do justice to the town of Bilbao if I could believe it possible that they would withhold this indulgence from the wives of the officers of the British army, more particularly as I have reason to believe that in that, any more than in other towns in Spain, it is not easy to get lodgings fit for the reception of respectable females; and that I would have every reason to hope that those ladies, feeling that they owe the accommodation they possess in the town to the desire of the town to gratify the officers of the British army, will on their parts, refrain from giving any cause for future complaint.

I cannot expect the Ayuntamiento will grant this indulgence to women not married; indeed I am astonished that any officer should have ventured to ask for billets for such persons; and I beg that in future a quarter may not be granted to any woman with an officer or to any lady singly, unless the military commandant of the hospital should certify that she is the wife of an officer.

There is no reason whatever, also why the wives of non-commissioned officers and soldiers of the army should be quartered in the houses with the officers of the army, unless their husbands should be in the house as the servant or orderly of the officer in

question; and, in case there should be any of that description, I beg
you to apply for the interference of the military commandant of the
hospital to have them removed to their husbands.

Letter from the commander of the forces to the Junta of Bilbao

J

1809. Soldiers' Marriages.

This subject requires much arrangement and attention and re-
ceives none. It affects the health, morality, and strength of our
army in various ways; such as desertion, population and other
points. My general ideas shall be set down, but I have not
considered the subject much, nor am I able perhaps to discuss it
properly: an able man should, however, serve his country material-
ly by taking it in hand. Marriage should be encouraged, but no
woman should be allowed to embark with a service expedition.
Going to the colonies or foreign garrisons would be different.
Regiments should generally be stationary in England, keeping to
their own counties, in each of which a women's barrack should be
built, and a manufactury should be established, or at least some
means for industry with schools for the children. The boys educated for the army and the girls if they married soldiers, should
have a government portion. These barracks should have a superin-
tendent, to be also a barrack-master, with rank of captain, and
always an old or disabled officer. Under him the schoolmaster and
mistress, the former a retired officer or non-commissioned officer;
the latter a widow, or wife of a deserving retired officer or
non-commissioned officer, who would have obtained a commission
if he had remained in service. Thus would many children be well
reared for the army in military villages. Desertion would nearly
cease, the women would be too comfortable to behave ill, and the
men, mostly married, would not have money for drinking, and
would be more healthy: their wives, rescued from debauchery,
would have more and stronger children and their joint labour
would enable them to live well.

This arrangement for children is founded on a calculation made
by my father, and given to me by Mr Windham, at Mr Fox's desire:
it would show a great public saving, when the expense of the boys is

balanced against the bounty now given to an equal number of recruits with the expenses of sending them to regiments. The population would be increased instead of being reduced by the size of our army which would itself be augmented in numbers and efficiency by increase of health: we have now often twenty thousand men ill at once from debauchery! Increased also by the increased number of boys, for most soldiers' children now die for want of care. Then, having the regiments formed of two fighting and one recruiting battalion, always near your women's barracks, with very few officers and a reduced staff, the army should be kept complete; for the boys would supply common casualties, and to meet those of a severe campaign many men would enlist under such a system. Abolish flogging and they would almost pay a bounty instead of receiving one.

Note by Lieutenant-Colonel (later General Sir Charles) Napier when a student at the Military College. (Biography by Sir William Napier Vol I, page 242.)

K

Daily Rates of pay for Infantry Soldiers

	Old Coinage	Decimal Coinage
Sergeants	From 1/6 to 2/-	From 7½p to 10p
Corporals	1/-	5p
Drummers and fifers	1/-	5p
Privates	-/8p	3½p
In the cavalry pay was slightly higher:		
e.g. Mounted private		7½p
Dismounted private		5p

Standing Orders for the Army in Ireland 1794

In the Rifle Corps the laundress was paid -/5d (equivalent to 2p) per week for each individual bundle of soldier's washing.

NOTES

Full bibliographical details are given in the first note for each source, thereafter the note is abbreviated to author's surname and page reference. A full list of the works cited in the text can be found in the *Bibliography*.

Introduction

1. Granville Leveson Gower, *Private Correspondence*, 1781–1821 (Murray, 1916).
2. Ibid., I, 261.
3 Ibid., I, 264.
4. M. Sherer, *Recollections of the Peninsula* (1824) 17.
5. Ibid., 59.
6. J. Kincaid, *Adventures in the Rifle Brigade* (Maclaren, 1835) 148.
7. J. Anton, *A Military Life* (Lizar, 1846) 176–7.
8. Kincaid, *Adventures*, 18.

Chapter 1

1. Stanhope, *Notes on Conversations with the Duke of Wellington* (1888) 86.
2. W. Wheeler, *Letters* (Michael Joseph, 1951) 161.
3. F. Shelley, *Diary* (Murray, 1913) I, 102.

Chapter 2

1. J. Fortescue, *History of the British Army* (Macmillan, 1906–12) IV, 903–7.
2. J. Fuller, *Sir John Moore's System of Training* (Hutchinson, 1924) 159.
3. Ibid., 160–1.

4. J. Donaldson, *Recollections of an Eventful Life* (Martin, 1852) 53–4.
5. Ibid., 39.
6. Fuller, 160.
7. Anton, 175.
8. G. Gleig, *The Subaltern* (Blackwood, 1825) 6–7.
9. Donaldson, 54.
10. Gleig, 9–19.
11. W. Surtees, *Twenty-Five Years in the Rifle Brigade* (Blackwood, 1833) 73, 101, 414.
12. Donaldson, 55, 152.
13. J. Harris, *Recollections* (London, 1848) 67–72.
14. J. Shipp, *Memoirs of an Extraordinary Career* (Fisher Unwin, 1890) 54–6.
15. H. Maxwell, *Life of Wellington* (Sampson Low, 1900) I, 18.
16. Donaldson, 48.
17. Anon, *Vicissitudes in the Life of a Scottish Soldier* (Colburn, 1827) 6.
18. Ibid., 6.
19. Anon., *Adventures of a Young Rifleman* (Colburn, 1826) 321.
20. Anon., *Vicissitudes*, 6–7 and E. Costello, *The Adventures of a Soldier* (1857) 7.

Chapter 3
1. J. Moore, *Diary of Sir John Moore* (Arnold, 1904) I, 371.
2. Anton, 174.
3. E. Wheatley, *The Wheatley Diary* (Longmans, 1964) 18.
4. Wheeler, 111.
5. Kincaid, *Adventures*, 22.
6. Sherer, 101.
7. Donaldson, 61.
8. R. Blakeney, *A Boy in the Peninsula* (Murray, 1899) 50.
9. Lady Burghclere, *A Great Man's Friendship* (Murray, 1927) 110.
10. B. O'Meara, *Napoleon in Exile* (Simpkin, 1822) II, 50.
11. C. Mercer, *Waterloo Campaign* (Blackwood, 1870) II, 3.
12. Wheeler, 103.
13. Costello, 142.
14. Anon., *Adventures*, 143.
15. Wheeler, 99.
16. Blakeney, 214.

17. F. Larpent, *Private Journals* (Bentley, 1853) I, 73.
18. Costello, 142.

Chapter 4

1. Anton, 44–5.
2. Ibid., 47–8.
3. Ibid., 61.
4. Ibid., 98–9.
5. Ibid., 114–15.
6. Ibid., 180.
7. Ibid., 208.
8. Ibid., 223.
9. Ibid., 234.

Chapter 5

1. Harris, 163.
2. Grattan, *Adventures in the Connaught Rangers* (1847) 145.
3. Gleig, 121–2.
4. Surtees, 146–7.
5. Harris, 31.
6. Sergeant Bourgogne, *Memoirs of Sergeant Bourgogne* (Peter Davis, 1926), 279.
7. Gleig, 122.
8. Donaldson, 360.
9. Anon., *Adventures*, 369.
10. W. Henry, *Events of a Military Life* (Pickering, 1843) 168–9.
11. W. Napier, *History of the Peninsular War* (Warne, 1886) III, 28.
12. de Marbot, *Memoirs* (Longmans, 1894) 426.
13. Blakeney, 314.
14. Costello, 173-4.
15. Ibid., 173–4.
16. Anton, 136.
17. Gleig, 333–5.
18. Wheeler, 140.
19. Ibid.
20. W. Tomkinson, *Diary of a Cavalry Officer* (Swann Sonnerschein, 1894) 188.
21. Napier, IV, 276.
22. Donaldson, 359.

23. Ibid., 74.
24. Ibid., 360.
25. Charles Oman, *History of the Peninsular War*, (1902) I, 154.

Chapter 6

1. Costello, 126–9.
2. A. Schaumann, *On the Road with Wellington* (Heinemann, 1924) 221–2.
3. Larpent, III, 211–13.
4. Anon., *Adventures* , 397–9.
5. F. Shelley, *Diary* (Murray, 1913) I, 49.
6. G. Bell, *Rough Notes of an Old Soldier* (1867)
7. C. Eaton, *Waterloo Days* (1888) 153.
8. Harris, 138.

Chapter 7

1. Wheeler, 97–8.
2. Ibid., 72.
3. Larpent, III, 174.
4. Gronow, *Reminiscences and Recollections* (Nimmo, 1889) 65.
5. Anon., *Vicissitudes*, 249.
6. Schaumann, 386.
7. Sherer, 89.
8. Schaumann, 82–3.
9. Kincaid, *Random Shots*, 204–7.
10. Anon., *Vicissitudes*, 305–7.
11. Harris, 100–3.
12. Schaumann, 29.
13. Kincaid, *Random Shots*, 32.
14. Ibid., 224.
15. Sherer, 99.
16. Kincaid, *Random Shots*, 32.
17. Tomkinson, 153.
18. W. Surtees, 313–4.
19. Anon., *A Soldier of the 71st or Glasgow Regiment* (Edinburgh, 1819) 177.
20. Schaumann, 336–40.
21. Larpent, I, 113–17.
22. Henry, 47–50.

23. Blakeney, 282–5.

24. Ibid., 290–4.

25. Kincaid, *Random Shots*, 61–2.

26. Schaumann, 207.

27. Blakeney, 207–8.

28. Henry, 83.

29. Ibid., 82–7.

30 Ibid., 82–7

31 Costello, 139–40, 202–13.

32. Wheeler, 113.

33. Bourgogne, 217.

34. Donaldson, 204.

35. Costello, 186.

36. Kincaid, *Random Shots*, 148.

37. Surtees, 317.

Chapter 8

1. H. Smith, *Autobiography* (Murray, 1910) 68.

2. Napier, IV, 113.

3. Donaldson, 158.

4. Smith, 218.

5. Ibid., 85.

6. Ibid., 95.

7. Ibid., 102.

8. Ibid., 115.

9. Ibid., 116.

10. Ibid., 133.

11. Ibid., 168.

12. Ibid., 292.

Chapter 9

1. Wheeler, 141.

2. Donaldson, 219.

3. Harris, 186–7.

4. J. Colville, *Portrait of a General* (Michael Russell, 1980) 108.

5. Harris, 194–5.

6. Bourgogne, 66.

7. Donaldson, 181–2.

8. Harris, 196–200.

9. Ibid., 139.
10. Ibid., 142.
11. Ibid., 137–44.
12. Donaldson, 224–5.
13. Wheeler, 153.
14. Donaldson, 224–5.

Chapter 10

1. Letter of 27 June 1811.
2. Napoleon Bonaparte, *Memoirs* (Hutchinson, n.d.) 152–7.
3. Wheeler, 187.
4. Henry, 24–7.
5. Sherer, 98–9.
6. Wheeler, 149–53, 189.
7. Schaumann, chapters 19–22; Smith, 90.

Chapter 11

1. T. Creevey, *The Creevey Papers* (Murray, 1927) 289.
2. Carola Oman, *The Gasgoyne Heiress* (Hodder and Stoughton, 1968) 260.
3. Eaton, 21.
4. Gronow, *Reminiscences and Recollections* (Nimmo, 1889) 186.
5. Tomkinson, 319.
6. E. Cotton, *A Voice from Waterloo* (1895), 138.

BIBLIOGRAPHY

Anon., *Adventures of a Young Rifleman*. Colburn, 1826.

Anon., *Vicissitudes in the Life of a Scottish Soldier*. Colburn, 1827.

Anon., *A Soldier of the 71st or Glasgow Regiment*. 1819.

Anton, J., *A Military Life*. Lizar, 1846.

Bell, G., *Rough Notes of an Old Soldier*. 1867.

Blakeney, R., *A Boy in the Peninsula*. Murray, 1899.

Bourgogne, Sergeant, *Memoirs of Sergeant Bourgogne*. Peter Davis, 1926.

Burghclere, Lady, *A Great Man's Friendship*. Murray, 1927.

Colville, J., *Portrait of a General*. Michael Russell, 1980.

Costello, E., *The Adventures of a Soldier*. 1857.

Cotton, E., *A Voice from Waterloo*. 1895.

Creevey, T., *The Creevey Papers*. Murray, 1905.

de Lancey, M., *A Week at Waterloo*. Murray, 1906.

Donaldson, J., *Recollections of an Eventful Life*. Martin, 1852.

Eaton, C., *Waterloo Days*. 1888.

Fortescue, J., *History of the British Army*, Volumes 4–7. Macmillan, 1906–12.

Fuller, J., *Sir John Moore's System of Training*. Hutchinson, 1924.

Gleig, G., *The Subaltern*. Blackwood, 1825.

Granville Leveson Gower, *Private Correspondence*, 1781–1821. Murray, 1916.

Grattan, *Adventures in the Connaught Rangers*. 1847.

Gronow, *Reminiscences and Recollections*. Nimmo, 1889.

Harris, J., *Recollections*. 1848.

Henry, W., *Events of a Military Life*. Pickering, 1843.

Kincaid, J., *Adventures in the Rifle Brigade*. Maclaren, 1835. *Random-Shots of a Rifleman*. 1835.

Larpent, F., *Private Journals*. Bentley, 1853.

Marbot de, *Memoirs*. Longmans, 1894.

Maxwell, H., *Life of Wellington*. Sampson Low, 1900.

Mercer, C., *Waterloo Campaign*. Blackwood, 1870.

Moore, J., *Diary of Sir John Moore*. Arnold, 1904.

Napier, W., *History of the Peninsular War*. Warne, 1886.

Napoleon Bonaparte, *Memoirs*, Hutchinson, n.d.

Oman, Charles, *History of the Peninsular War*, Volume I. 1902.

Oman, Carola, *The Gasgoyne Heiress*. Hodder and Stoughton, 1968.

O'Meara, B., *Napoleon in Exile*. Simpkin, 1822.

Schaumann, A., *On the Road with Wellington*. Heinemann, 1924.

Sherer, M., *Recollections of the Peninsula*. 1824.

Shelley, F., *Diary*. Murray, 1913.

Shipp, J., *Memoirs of an Extraordinary Career*. Fisher Unwin, 1890.

Smith, H., *Autobiography*. Murray, 1910.

Stanhope, E., *Notes on Conversations with the Duke of Wellington*. 1888.

Surtees, W., *Twenty Five Years in the Rifle Brigade*. Blackwood, 1833.

Tomkinson, W., *Diary of a Cavalry Officer*. Swan Sonnerschein 1894.

Duke of Wellington, *Standing Orders*, 1832.

Wheatley, E., *The Wheatley Diary*. Longmans, 1964.

Wheeler, W., *Letters*. Michael Joseph, 1951.

Standing Orders and Regulations for the Army in Ireland, 1794.

Regulations and Orders for the Army, 1816.

Rules and Regulations for the Cavalry, 1795.

INDEX

Lowe, Sir Hudson 118-19

MacCullogh, Lieutenant 70-1
MacDermot, Nancy 54
McGuire, Mr. and Mrs. 100-1
McKenzie, General 125-6
Maibee, Sergeant and Mrs. 32-3
Marbot, General 51-2
Masséna, Marshal 9-10
Mercer, C: *Waterloo Campaign* 31-2
Mitchell, Captain 122-4
Montgomery, Field-Marshal: *A History of
    Warfare* 45-6
Moore, Sir John 6-7, 26, 48, 104

Napier, Sir W: *History of the Peninsular War*
    57, 88, 139-40
Napoleon Bonaparte 5, 11-14
    on women 31, 109
Ney, Marshal 9
Nightingale, Florence 131
nuns and the Peninsular War 72-3, 111-12

Packenham, Sir Edward 97, 136-7
Paget, Edward 22
Palafox, General 6, 59
pay for infantry soldiers 140
Peninsular War 2-3, 5-14, 27-44, 48-59,
    87-94, 100-8
Picton, Sir Thomas 67-8
Pipin, Corporal 112-13
Pitt, William 15
Pullen, Rifleman and Mrs. 104-5

Quatre Bras, battle of 14, 122

Reston, Sergeant and Mrs. 57-9
Richmond, Duchess of – her ball 14, 45,
    119-21
Rules and Regulations for the Cavalry (1795)
    (on marriage) 15

Salamanca, battle of 11, 89
Sale, Lady 130
Schaumann, Augustus: *On the Road* 68-74
    passim, 82, 102
    and Maria Josepha 114-17
Scott, Walter 128
Shelley, F: *Diary* 65

Sherer, M: *Recollections* 3, 29-30, 69, 73, 112
Shipp, John: *Memoirs* 22
Siego, Maria Josepha 91, 113-17
Skiddy, Mrs. 66
Smith, Harry 88-99, 117
Smith, Juana Maria, 88-99, 117
Soult, Marshal 8-9, 11, 50-1
Stewart, Duncan and Mary 19-20
Sturt, Lieutenant and Mrs. 130-1
Suchet, Marshal 11, 12
Surtees, W: *Twenty-Five Years in the Rifle
    Brigade* 20-1, 49, 73-4, 86

thwarted love 76-80
'to-go' or 'not-to-go' tickets 17-18, 36
Tomkinson, W: *Diary* 56-7, 73, 123
Torres Vedras, Lines of 9-11

Vandeleur, General 76, 93
Victor, Marshal 9
Vitoria, Battle of 12, 50, 92

Waterloo campaign 13-14, 26-7, 31, 66,
    120-8
Wellesley *see* Wellington
Wellington, Duke of 75-6, 118-19, 130
    campaigns
        Peninsular War 6-12, 56
        Waterloo 13-14, 120-2, 127
    and Duchess of Richmond's ball 45-6,
        121
    and women 31, 67, 69, 109
        General Orders (concerning women)
            133-5, 137
        letters (concerning women) 135-6,
            137-9
West, Private 89, 91, 98-9
Wheatley, E: *Diary* 28
Wheeler, W: *Letters* 13, 28, 56, 67, 84, 100,
    112-13
women
    on the battlefield 48-59, 66
    heroism 56-9, 65, 96
    masquerading as men 129-30
    misdeeds on campaigns 30-1, 55
    pregnancy in the field 100-3
    sale of wives 50, 62
    widowed in the field 49-50
    see also conditions for women